Waterford Whispers News
2024

COLM WILLIAMSON

Gill Books

Gill Books
Hume Avenue
Park West
Dublin 12
www.gillbooks.ie

Gill Books is an imprint of M.H. Gill & Co.

© Colm Williamson 2024

978 07171 9725 5

Designed by seagulls.net
Copy-edited by Liza Costello
Proofread by Jane Rogers
Printed and bound in Spain by GraphyCems

*Waterford Whispers News* is a satirical newspaper and comedy website published by Waterford Whispers News. Waterford Whispers News uses invented names in all the stories in this book, except in cases when public figures are being satirised. Any other use of real names is accidental and coincidental.

For permission to reproduce photographs, the author and publisher gratefully acknowledge the following:
© Adobe Stock: Aleksandr Lesik, 56; alfa27, 126; All king of people, 93; Andy Dean, 38R; Angelov, 125T; anko, 129B; annanahabed, 121T; AntonioDiaz, 106; ARVD73, 40L; athichoke.pim, 132T; Auremar, 111T; AZP Worldwide, 54L; Bartu, 33L; Beaunitta V W, 141; Brent Hofacker, 168; BullRun, 36L; bunyos, 53F; ChasingMagic, 43T; ColleenMichaels, 152B; Cookie Studio, 92B, 10L; Dahi, 116L; Daxiao Productions, 128; Denis Boyko, 45R; deagreez, 120, 104T; diquesvet, 33R; Dolores Harvey, 87R; Drazen, 158B; Drobot Dean, 112; Duncan Andison, 146B; dusanpetkovic1, 43B; espiegle, 146T; FiledIMAGE, 130B; fizkes, 157T, 101T, 131; Flamingo Images, 108; fesenko, 36; funkenzauber, 159L; Goodluz, 124; Gumirova Elvira, 52R; Halfpoint, 79B; Highwaystarz, 41; Hunor Kristo, 80L; Iliya Mitskavets, 151B; Insta_photos, 57; JackF, 107, 129T; Jale Ibrak, 32; Jeremy, 120; Joaquin Corbalan, 137; Jose Calsina, 48; kamilpetran, 151T; kostyha, 92T; Krakenimages.com, 104B, 20; Kzenon, 114L, 135B, 166; lisinama, 82; Mark Gusev, 29L; Massimo Todaro, 28; Mdv Edwards, 110; MIKHAIL, 150; Monkey Business, 44, 117, 123; Moodboard, 114R; Mr Doomits, 67T; nata_rass, 94; Nejron Photo, 30; New Africa, 89B, 171; Nicoletaionescu, 115; Nomad_Soul, 140; Noraismail, 61; Oleksandr, 15L; OSORIOartist, 71; Patcharanan, 165; Pathdoc, 46; Pawelsierakowski, 45; Petro, 138; phonlamaiphoto, 8; Photographee.eu, 162; Photology1971, 23; Postmodern Studio, 155L; Prostock-Studio, 87; Rh2010, 102; Rido, 29R; Seventyfour, 5; Serghi8, 73; Shawn, 49T; Sinseeho, 164; Skif, 42; sofiko14, 26; Soupstock, 40; Sriba3, 163; Stephen, 15R, 13; Studio Romantic, 145R; Syda Productions, 125B, 50; TheVisualsYouNeed, 79T; Tsuguliev, 130T; Tupungato, 170; Tyler Olson, 133; WavebreakmediaMicro, 152T, 156; Wirestock, 22; Yakobchuk Olena, 99; Yelantsevv, 59R; Yuliia, 126, 101B; Yuri Arcurs, 98, 109; © Alamy: AJ Pics, 12C; aphperspective, 83; BFA, 93R; Bob Pardue – SC, 154; Clearpix, 134; Imago, 65; JOHN BRACEGIRDLE, 63L; Jeremy Pembrey, 139B; Justin Ng, 19B; nidpor / StockimoNews, 80B; PA Images, 6, 10, 27, 91B, 132B, 139B; Patti McConville, 27; Tommy London, 81; Xinhua, 45; WENN Rights Ltd, 80T; © Flickr: Paul Reynolds: 11L; © Getty: AFP, 39B; Charles McQuillan, 21; Dáire Brennan / Sportsfile, 136T; Hasan Mrad / UCG / Universal Images, 142; Martin Sylvest Andersen, 96; Ramsey Cardy, 139T; renphotos, 116B; © Reuters: 62; © Shutterstock: Adam Schultz, 90C; AfriramPOE, 54; akramalrasny, 68B; akramalrasny, 73; Alexandros Michailidis, 12L, 23, 61, 67B; Alexandre Prevot, 122; Anas-Mohammed, 17; BANDZRIO, 48L; B. Lenoir, 86; bookzv, 84; Bumble Dee, 63R; BublikHaus, 47; BMPhotolab, 113; Claire Whitehead, 49B; Damien Storan, 4, 7T, 11R, 19T, 91T; D. Ribeiro, 44R, 95, 135; Darya Chacheva, 85B; Dfree, 90(2TR), 90TL; Derick P. Hudson, 16, 153L; DGLimages, 31R; Elnur, 96L; frank333, 118, 155R, ; Featureflash Photo Agency, 90BR; Fred Duavl, 90 (2BR), 90TR, 137L; gdvcom, 145L; Keith Homan, 157B; LCV, 84; Lenscap Photography, 86; lensmen, 9; lev radin, 59L, 90(2BL), 90BL; LiamMurphyPics, 18, 34, 38, 58T; lovelypeace, 37; Maverick Pictures, 68T; Mark Reinstein, 72L; Monkey Business, 45; noel bennett, 160; Paul Burr, 147; Paul Froggatt, 72R; peace-loving, 78; photocosmos1, 12R; Prashantrajsingh, 66, 70; RadulePerisic, 35; Roman Nerud, 100; rblfmr, 74; Sergey Denisenko, 159; Stefano Chiacchiarini '74, 89T; teera.noisakran, 114C; Tinseltown, 90(2TL); tubuceo, 64; Vershinin89, 158T; Vianney Le Caer, 88; Zoteva, 151B. © RollingNews.ie: Leah Farrell, 32, 52L; © Wikimedia Commons: Batoul84, 39T; Gage Skidmore, 75; William Murphy, 85T.

The author and publisher have made every effort to trace all copyright holders, but if any have been inadvertently overlooked we would be pleased to make the necessary arrangement at the first opportunity.

The paper used in this book comes from the wood pulp of sustainably managed forests.

All rights reserved.

No part of this publication may be copied, reproduced or transmitted in any form or by any means, without written permission of the publishers.

A CIP catalogue record for this book is available from the British Library.

5 4 3 2 1

# CONTENTS

| | |
|---|---:|
| **LETTER FROM THE EDITOR** | 1 |
| **POLITICS** | 3 |
| **LOCAL NEWS** | 25 |
| **WORLD NEWS** | 55 |
| **ENTERTAINMENT** | 77 |
| **LIFESTYLE** | 97 |
| **SPORT** | 127 |
| **PROPERTY** | 143 |
| **BUSINESS** | 149 |
| ***WWN* GUIDES** | 161 |

**Colm Williamson** created *Waterford Whispers News* in 2009 when he was made unemployed during the financial crash. Though it began as a hobby, with Colm sharing stories with family and friends, his unique brand of topical, distinctly Irish satire quickly attracted thousands of fans. Now *Waterford Whispers News* has over 1 million followers across social media platforms. *WWN* has performed live shows everywhere from LA to the 3Arena. Accolades include being banned from RTÉ before it was cool after the last appearance sparked protests and over 6,000 complaints from the public. Not content with conquering satire, *WWN* launched an online merchandise shop at waterfordwhispers.shop earlier this year. Colm runs *Waterford Whispers News* from his home town of Tramore in County Waterford.

# LETTER FROM THE EDITOR

Thank you, dear reader, for purchasing this weighty tome full of the most incisive wisdom since Daniel O'Donnell's *Guide To Altering The Wills Of Your Elderly Fans & Getting Away With It*.

Some say we're teetering on the very edge of the precipice of the cliff face of a dark, dark chapter in humanity's fast-accelerating demise. I say that's a lot of words when you can just say, 'humanity's fucked'.

I also say that's a very negative way to speak of 2024, a fine year which gave us the Willy Wonka Experience in Glasgow, the breakdancer Raygun and Brat summer. Even the politicians up the North went to couples counselling. What a lovely positive year for everyone except Donald Trump's earlobe.

Personally, I've never had a better year: I was elected councillor in this year's local elections, benefitting from being the only non-head-the-ball in the field.

As you know, Bill Badbody isn't just the editor of *Waterford Whispers News*, I'm a man who wears many hats or, in the case of evicting a 92-year-old tenant who refuses to pay €2000 a month in rent, a balaclava.

I'm a businessman. That's too humble; I'm a business God.

Ireland Inc. couldn't be healthier, business is booming. Debt collectors are having to hire extra heavies to keep up with the demand for repossessions of local businesses. And if you're in the business of cleaning up and refurbing properties after racists have set them on fire, I don't need to tell you what a great year you've had.

I can't tell you the money I've made on insurance payouts after starting rumours a property I own was being converted into accommodation. No really, on the advice of my lawyers I literally cannot tell you.

My efforts to get the fencing contract for the Grand Canal tent city were hindered by my closest rival as he literally fenced in my car, so I was late to my meeting with the Minister for Lucrative State Contracts. That blow was softened somewhat when I was asked to provide a bike shed for Leinster House.

The Ireland of 2024 is very much like those funny optical illusions where it's a drawing of a beautiful young woman but when you turn it upside down it's a hideously decaying old woman of about 50. If, like me, you've got a bit of moola, Ireland is just swell and anyone suggesting an upheaval in the order of things is clearly just looking at things all gee-eyed. In fairness, you'd have to be drunk and seeing things to think Ireland is a country of growing inequality in which people struggle to survive.

Our prosperity really puts things in perspective. I sometimes think, what's the point in a general election at all when things are this good under The TikTokseach? And then I remember if I win a seat I get free travel on the gravy train for life.

Yours factually,

Bill Badbody

Deputy stand-in temporary editor of *WWN*, landlord, local councilor, philanthropist and man of the people.

POLITICS

Waterford Whispers News

**REFERENDUM**

# GOVERNMENT ADMITS FAILURE OF THICK-AS-SHIT PUBLIC TO UNDERSTAND REFERENDUMS

SIFTING through the wreckage of Friday's two unsuccessful referendums, the Irish coalition government is now openly admitting its failures, chiefly how it has to contend with the fact it wholeheartedly underestimated the levels of brain rot present amongst the great unwashed.

'Sometimes you've got to hold your hands up and admit you knew the Irish public were stupid but not this stupid. We can admit when we're wrong, and we got it so wrong here, you thickos can't even grasp our amazing referendum messaging and campaigning,' confirmed a spokesperson from the Government.

'Mea culpa, our bad. We knew our messaging was clear and concise but we should have boiled it down to monosyllabic grunts for you guys,' confirmed the taoiseach, who said he couldn't rule out future voting ballots being made of Play-Doh.

The resounding rejection of the Government's wording for the two amendments to the Constitution has led to a radical reappraisal of how the voting public is perceived in some political circles.

'Aaaaàm I speeeeeaking slooooooowly enoooooough, do you understand?' confirmed the new head of the Government's Thick-As-Shit-Public Liaison Unit, which will lead a €20m marketing drive to explain why

> 'Sometimes you've got to hold your hands up and admit you knew the Irish public were stupid'

**Did You Know?**

For the barren desert scenes in *Dune: Part Two*, director Denis Villeneuve filmed on location in Kilkenny.

the public should apologise to the Government.

Similarly astute observations made by conservative elements in Irish society have confirmed that the No–No vote, with a turnout of 44.4%, is proof Irish people want a swift return to the Utopian times of 1950s Ireland.

Elsewhere, Sinn Féin have emerged from their referendum hibernation to confirm that the public can trust their party to communicate clearly with them, which is why they're now trying to pretend like they didn't say they would re-run a reworded care referendum if a No vote was successful.

Politics

## MENTAL HEALTH

# HSE URGES CHILDREN TO GROW OUT OF MENTAL HEALTH ISSUES AND GET ON WITH IT LIKE EVERYONE ELSE

'IT'S far from a functioning mental health service you were reared,' was the line a HSE spokesperson told parents of children waiting over two years to be seen by psychiatrists following news today of yet more failures from the €21bn per year shitshow.

'We're also really sorry we can't reopen an 11-bed ward at the Linn Dara Child and Adolescent Mental Health Services inpatient unit, but we can't find the staff to underpay and work to the bone – it's like nurses these days are becoming too big for their boots, looking for a living wage and standard working conditions,' the HSE added, having recently admitted to paying eight HSE staff members more than half a million euro last year.

With a list of scandals that would take the same four-month time period to read as it would a child waiting to get vital spinal surgery, the HSE suggested to children waiting up to two years for mental health services to not hold their breath, and to just grow out of any mental health issues they may have like everyone else has had to do in Ireland for the past forever.

'There are plenty of mental health podcasts out there you could listen to,' the spokesperson went on. 'Blindboy, Bressie, that lad who left Today FM; sure, ye're spoiled rotten these days with options.'

'Maybe go for a little run or a swim in the sea, be grand,' he concluded, before going on a two-hour lunch break.

### Famous Quotes from 2024

"Wow, people weren't kidding; the flames down here are VERY hot"
- OJ Simpson

Waterford Whispers News

## THE MIDDLE EAST

# 'DON'T GO, YOU'RE GREAT CRAIC' – IRELAND REACTS TO THE ISRAELI AMBASSADOR RECALL

FOLLOWING news that Israel's Ambassador to Ireland, Dana Erlich, has been recalled over Ireland's decision to recognise the state of Palestine, *WWN* takes to the streets to get local reactions.

'She'll probably insist on taking someone's window seat on the plane.'
– John from Portlaw

'Is the Israeli embassy up for rent now or what?'
– Julie from Leitrim

'Recalled? I knew she had a few faults alright.'
– Tim from Tralee

'Don't let the door hit her arse on the way out, as they'll probably fucking bomb the shit out of us if it does.'
– Mark, Clonmel

'That'll hurt Israel's Irish televote score in the Eurovision next year.'
– Ciaran, Galway

'She has a face on her that'd stop all the clocks in Switzerland, so best they fly around.'
– Martin, pilot, Dublin Airport

'Aw don't go, Dana, you're great craic.'
– Several people speaking at the same time

'Ah feck's sake, it was her turn to host our book club.'
– Alan, Dublin

'Can she take Alan Shitter with her?'
– Dave, Tramore

'I think I'll miss her defence of the mass murder of innocent civilians the most.'
– Bernie, Dublin

'Just make sure she doesn't take any Irish passports with her on her way out.'
– Mark, Wicklow

'Does anyone know if she had Europa League final tickets, and if so, can I have them now?'
– Tony, Cork

'And another thing – Guinness is shite, Tayto smells like feet and is owned by Germans. The Cliffs of Moher? Tiny in person, boring even. I'm out!'
– Dana Erlich, former Israeli ambassador to Ireland

Politics

## CYBER CRIME

## 'IT WAS HANDY ENOUGH' – MEET THE MAN WHO HACKED THE HSE

WHIZZ KID IT security adviser Alan Hodgkins may look like your ordinary everyday pensioner, but on weekends the Waterford man likes to test government databases for fun.

'Bought this baby back at the turn of the century and still runs Windows '98 like a dream,' the 84-year-old self-confessed hacker told *WWN*, before demonstrating how he manages to breach a range of networks containing vital personal information.

'I'm in the mainframe!' Hodgkins exclaimed, now showing this reporter how easy it was to break into an unnamed government system, much like the Covid-related database he breached in December of 2021, opening up the details of more than a million people to potential exploitation.

'Password was "Covid-19", so once I was in, I immediately got on to the HSE to tell them they were vulnerable, as I'm not a bad hacker,' he added of the breach, which the HSE only reported to the Data Protection Commissioner (DPC) last week, some two years after the fact 'because Ireland'.

'They're nearly as fast-acting as my 56kps dial-up modem,' he pointed out. 'Good thing it was only the names, addresses and personal health details of over one million people or this would have been very embarrassing for them, especially after all the other hacking incidents since then.

'At least it wasn't the details of anyone important, just normal everyday Joe Soaps during Covid at a time when all GDPR seemed to be thrown out the window anyway, so fair game as far as the Government is concerned.'

In response, the minister of defence Simon Coveney has increased the paper clip budget for the National Cyber Security Centre by €3.45.

### 2025 Predictions

After a successful pilot scheme, North Korea is to give internet access to a second citizen.

## BREAKING

## VARADKAR RESIGNS AFTER ACHIEVING DREAM OF RECORD HOMELESSNESS

FINE GAEL leader since 2017 and current taoiseach, Leo Varadkar has just announced his resignation on the steps of Leinster House.

Speaking to the assembled media just moments ago, an emotional Varadkar explained the shocking decision, which has been described as a political earthquake:

'And Alexander wept as he had no more worlds to conquer, no more inequality to exacerbate, no more data centres to build, no more tents to destroy while busing asylum seekers to the Dublin Mountains, no more Mother and Baby Home survivors to leave out of a redress scheme, no more tax rebates to give for developers, no more Children's Hospital budgets to balloon to the size of a small moon, no more waiting lists to extend, no more nurses and teachers to drive to the airport for emigration, no more hoteliers to enrich with state contracts and no political failures left to blame on the opposition for the fiftieth time.'

7

Waterford Whispers News

## EURO ELECTIONS
# SACK OF GANGRENOUS PUS ANNOUNCES MEP BID

A LARGE sack of gangrenous puss grown in a lab by scientists has announced its bid for the European elections, *WWN* reports.

The putrid pile of steaming infection has been tipped by bookies to gain a seat after the scientists revealed it could also spout right-leaning soundbites on command and already has a huge following online since its growth.

'We programmed it to use keywords and phrases like 'unvetted military-aged males' and within minutes it had reached over 200,000 followers on Telegram, so we then put it forward for selection to become a candidate in the MEP elections and voila,' lead scientist behind the project Adolf O'Brien told *WWN*.

Competing with a range of similar candidates from across the country, the foul-smelling bag of festering pus will have a tough race but is confident it will do well this July.

'Black Muslim transgender grooming paedophile gangs with barbed penises,' the gangrenous bag uttered from its opening, which resembled a skydiver's mouth. 'Irish for the Ireland ... cheese grater replacement ... climate spare change please ... two euro for the bus ... let's all wear camo and be racist in the woods while secretly having homoerotic thoughts.'

'Ahem ... obviously, we're having some teething problems with its vocab, but we're pretty confident spluttering incoherent soundbites that only a simpleton could derive meaning from won't hurt Pus Bag's chances at all,' inventor O'Brien concluded.

### 2025 Predictions
The Sinn Féin government will nationalise children's piggy banks and make it illegal to own your own home.

### Famous Quotes from 2024
"No, please, whatever you've heard it's not true, just a rumour spread on Telegram" - **derelict building, shortly before being set on fire**

Politics

## ROAD SAFETY

# IRISH PEOPLE GIVE THEIR SOLUTIONS TO REDUCING ROAD FATALITIES

CALLS continue for authorities to step in and improve the situation on Irish roads amid an uptick in fatal collisions.

WWN took to the streets to hear from the Irish people and garner their opinions on solutions to help reduce road fatalities.

'Clamp down on drink driving, but let lads who are grand driving after a few pints tip on home.'
– **John Tierney, Rural Drivers Association**

'No, no, you're grand, I can take a call, the M50 is quiet enough. A survey, is it? Yeah, go on.'
– **Dave Cartlin, ambulance driver**

'Dress school kids in clothes made out of airbags, problem solved.'
– **Noreen Hughes, cataract sufferer**

'Bring back the Samantha Mumba ad!'
– **Grace Tallon, advertising executive**

'Trying to avoid unnecessary road deaths in any way is just a scam by grieving families to get more money in the coffers of Revenue through fines.'
– **Sean Kingley, disqualified driver**

'The public learned through a Freedom of Information request that garda detections of mobile use by drivers were down 40%, stopped for speeding down 30% and drink driving arrests down by 14% compared to 2019 figures, so maybe we should make it harder for people to do Freedom of Information requests?'
– **Drew Harris, Garda Commissioner**

'If I buy a bigger SUV then I'll survive any collision with an SUV, or a cyclist.'
– **Tara Pontin, SUV driver**

'Make everyone do a new driver test every five years. Except me, I'm class at driving.'
– **Cian Breen, driving instructor**

'Just fine Audi drivers the second they buy an Audi, cut out the middle man.'
– **Cristina Sanchez, jealous pedestrian**

'Keeping the maximum sentence for careless driving causing death at two years is brilliant, don't change that.'
– **Greg O'Carolan, speed limit breaker**

### Did You Know?
In a couple of decades historians will be calling the current time period you're living through 'World War III'.

Waterford Whispers News

## HEALTH

# CHILD INITIALLY CHOSEN FOR CHILDREN'S HOSPITAL RIBBON-CUTTING CEREMONY TURNS 31

'SO MUCH HAS changed; I hit puberty, went to college, got married, had my own kids. Wow, I was so naive back then; not only did I think the hospital would be finished on time I thought it would cost €600m,' confirmed Rory Power, blowing out the candles on his birthday cake, the 21st birthday cake he has had since originally being ask to formally open the 'almost finished' hospital.

> 'I was so naive back then; not only did I think the hospital would be finished on time I thought it would cost €600m'

'I never thought I'd reach this age due to my ill health as a kid so I suppose I'll have to thank those who made that possible; the Spanish health service,' added Power.

Speaking before the Public Accounts Committee, hospital officials confirmed the hospital would definitely be finished by late next year, maybe, don't quote them on that, and probably operational the year after, but sure look, you know how these things go.

Power had confessed to hoping the initial offer to be the ribbon cutter was still open but appreciated it would not be a good look to have an adult doing it.

'The only worse choice for ribbon cutting would be a group of smiling politicians who sat idly by as taxpayers' money was set on fire and the budget ballooned, showing zero interest in holding the contractor to account,' concluded Power.

### County Council Notices

The annual fly-tipping jamboree will take place countywide at unknown locations. We would like to remind you to only dump your most toxic waste.

Politics

## TELEVISION

## NATION SENDS SIGNAL INTO SKY IN BID TO GET VINCENT BROWNE OUT OF RETIREMENT

A DESPERATE NATION in need of seeing their public representatives squirm in discomfort as their bolloxology is called out have raised an improvised bat-signal in the sky calling for a far greater hero than Batman; retired Irish broadcaster Vincent Browne.

'Shit-eating grins on all of them, they know they can get away with just talking in circles. Vincent, we need you,' pleaded the public, as it feels it can't take much more of politicians waffling to such an extent that they have rendered the English language meaningless.

Flourishing due to the inability of the media to them call out for the dearth of ideas, lack of specific details on policy proposals and constant evasion when clearly not answering the question they were asked, politicians remain so emboldened that the appearance of the old TV3 logo being burned into the night sky is the only hope for desperate Irish people.

'I just watch old clips on YouTube and pretend he's eviscerating Stephen Donnelly over the cost of the Children's Hospital rather than the fact he jumped ship to Fianna Fáil in a naked act of self-importance and lust for power for power's sake,' lamented one old *Tonight With Vincent Browne* viewer.

'Six years now and I miss his browbeating of meritless suits who think it's their divine right to poorly run the country,' added another, cradling a picture of Vincent Browne on his TV3 set close to his chest.

It is believed the beacon will remain lit in the sky until such a time that Browne grumpily gives in and returns to grilling politicians.

## VOTE

# VOTE: WHAT SHOULD SIMON HARRIS'S NICKNAME AS TAOISEACH BE?

AS HE TAKES power to a wave of adulation and confetti, Simon Harris, Ireland's youngest ever taoiseach, is in need of an era-defining nickname that reflects the universal warmth and acclaim which has greeted his ascension to the throne.

Indicating he is truly a man of the people, Simon Harris (who insisted we call him 'Si') won't grant the public a general election; however, he has entrusted *WWN* with securing him his nickname, and we're putting the responsibility in our readers' hands.

So, what should Simon Harris's nickname as taoiseach be?

**What should Simon Harris's nickname as taoiseach be?**
a) The Shock (submitted as a suggestion by Simon Harris)
b) The Talentless Mr Ripley
c) Leo Varadkar (Zero Sugar)
d) The TikTokSeach
e) Kendall Roy – Greystones Edition
f) Wicklow Pinocchio
g) He's not getting a nickname until all Mother and Baby Home survivors get redress and children needing spinal surgery get it as promised when he was minister for health. And that's just for starters.

11

Waterford Whispers News

# BREAKING

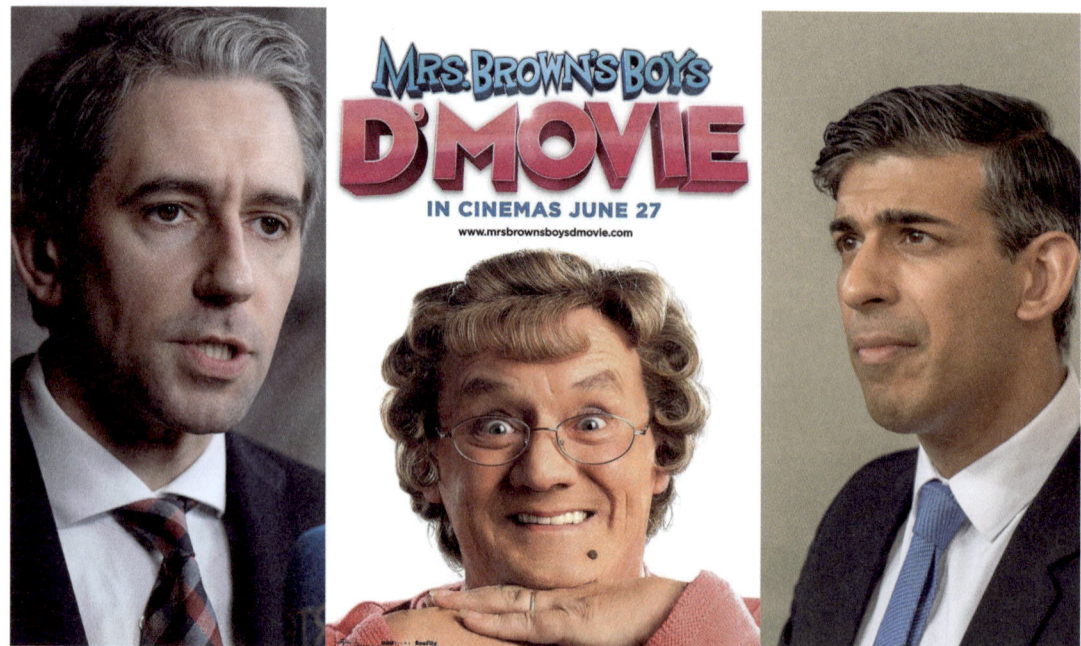

# IRISH GOVERNMENT THREATENS FUNDING 10 MORE SERIES OF *MRS BROWN'S BOYS* IN UK ASYLUM SEEKER ROW

IN A SIGN that the diplomatic row relating to asylum seekers between the Irish and British governments has entered its 'on the verge of nuclear war' phase, British Taoiseach Rishi Sunak has received a grave threat from the Irish government.

'Get every available officer in Northern Ireland on this, there's no time to lose, stop those asylum seekers crossing into Ireland. You, yes fucking you, chart 5,000 Ryanair flights from Dublin to London, pack 'em with refugees. No, no priority queuing, that'd bankrupt us,' a panicked Sunak said after Taoiseach Simon Harris threatened to directly fund new episodes of *Mrs Brown's Boys* for the BBC if the UK doesn't stem the flow of asylum seekers entering Ireland from the UK via Northern Ireland.

'And I thought us sending asylum seekers to Rwanda was the most heartless and evil act a politician was capable of, but that was until Harris said, "think about it, not just a Christmas Special episode, there will be an Easter one, King's Birthday special, Wimbledon special, autumn equinox special",' a stunned Sunak said to his staff in Downing Street.

As news spread of the threat from Ireland, terrified Britons sought shelter and threw their televisions out their windows, preemptively filling their ears with cement and gouging their eyes out.

Elsewhere, political commentators denied it would be advantageous to a struggling government party to suddenly pick a row on the issue of asylum seekers entering the country via Northern Ireland, something they have been aware of for years but have not acted on in any meaningful way.

## County Council Notices

New art installation displaying how much money the council had to spend on social housing but didn't bother its arse is now on display on the quay.

## Classifieds

**RAP ALBUM COLLECTIONS FOR SALE**

I'm currently selling all my P. Diddy, R. Kelly and Drake album collections and possibly a few more rap album vinyl collections in the near future. I recently started seeing a woman and need to sell these quickly so I can invite her over to stay the night.

Call Izzy on 089-56524547

Politics

ANALYSIS

# REASONS WHY A UNITED IRELAND COULD COST €20BN A YEAR

AN ANALYSIS by Dublin-based think tank the Institute of International and European Affairs puts the potential cost of a united Ireland at between €8bn and €20bn a year.

Since *WWN* is a self-respecting news publication you can trust we obviously led with the highest possible number in our headline. But just how exactly would the financial burden of a united Ireland hit such highs? We crunch the numbers below.

- Academics producing hypothetical studies based on speculative and pulled-from-arse data points regarding a united Ireland don't come cheap and will need to be paid frequently, and handsomely, if a united Ireland has any chance of being a success.
- Cost of flamethrowers required to burn all Nordie Tayto stock would run into the hundreds of millions.
- €260m: ear plugs for every citizen when 'Ireland's Call' is adopted as the official anthem of a united Ireland.
- Interpreter fees would skyrocket as civil servants north and south are forced to interact with one another.
- The increase in population would mean building an extension to the Children's Hospital, which would immediately swallow half the €20bn budget.
- A small increase of even just five in the number of additional TDs in the Dáil could cost the taxpayer €5bn in expenses claims alone.
- Deciding what to do with the additional tax revenue generated by an incoming 1.8m people will require paying billions to consultancy firms to figure out.
- The therapy required for Jamie Bryson will be considerable and come at great cost to the newly formed State.
- If, in the event of a Sinn Féin government in the Dáil, money will be spent on paying hardline nationalists in the 26 counties to ignore the fact they're now saddled with funding the £10bn the British government sends to Northern Ireland every year to plug its fiscal deficit.
- Every Irish road would have to be downgraded to match Northern Irish roads.
- Retraining obsolete fuel and contraband criminals in the border region will cost tens of millions.
- Draining Lough Neagh so its pollution is evenly spread out over the 32 counties will cost at least €4bn.
- Conjoining the HSE and the Northern Ireland NHS so that their respective dysfunctions sync up would be of huge cost. That's not even taking into account the thousands of middle-management positions required to make sure it's as inefficient and costly a process as humanly possible.
- Deaths from arguments over the design of the new flag could cost the State billions.

**Mindlessness Tip**
Buying a gratitude journal can help you appreciate the positive things in your life. How much? €25 for a fucking gratitude journal? Fuck that.

Waterford Whispers News

## HEALTH

# DEPARTMENT OF WELFARE WORKER SIGNED OFF FOR SIX MONTHS FOR STRESS AFTER BEING ASKED QUESTION

A HARROWING case of chronic on-the-job stress has been uncovered by *WWN*'s investigative unit after one social welfare recipient came forward with details of a troubling and emotionally challenging moment.

'One minute I was asking a question I thought was a fairly routine one on Jobseeker's Benefit, then suddenly the woman at the desk kinda went into a catatonic shock,' shared Jobseeker's recipient Donal Rattling.

What was unclear to Rattling in the moment was that welfare worker Sheila Wheatley's body was suddenly overwhelmed by the inquiry as, after years in the job, her body and mind had become so accustomed to a workload close to 'hammock tester' that any request to actually complete a task or answer a question could have proven fatal.

'She's still in a fragile state and isn't fit for being interviewed,' *WWN* was told by Wheatley's supervisor, who begged welfare recipients to be more mindful when interacting with staff.

'Think before you ask basic questions you'd expect any reasonable person to answer. The sense of entitlement some of you have, thinking you deserve an answer that didn't make you feel like you had somehow asked someone to walk backwards down the Grand Canyon while doing a Rubik's Cube. Shame on you,' confirmed the supervisor, shortly before being signed off themselves for 'life-endangering levels of interactions with the general public'.

### Classifieds

**TOMMY WANTED**

My name is Tommy and everyone says I'm gas craic. I'm looking for another hilarious fucker called Thomas, Tom or Tommy to start up a comedy duo/two-piece band called The 2 Tommies so we can make loads of money from being class. Must be able to sing, dance and crack jokes on a whim and be knowledgeable of the GAA and pop culture things like Wavin piping or custard creams lol. We're gonna be mental.

Call Tommy on 085-547858966

Politics

# POLLS

## POLL: WHICH MEMBER OF YOUR FAMILY SPRANG TO MIND WHEN YOU HEARD ASSISTED DYING COULD BE LEGALISED IN IRELAND?

WITH an Oireachtas committee report on assisted dying recommending that the government introduce legislation allowing the practice following nine months of debate and expert testimony, which member of your family immediately sprang to mind when you first learned of this news?

**Which Member of your Family Sprang to Mind when You Heard Assisted Dying could be Legalised in Ireland?**

a) She's my sister, I love her, but she says 'pacifically' instead of 'specifically'
b) Whichever one has the most road frontage
c) If I marry Mark Zuckerberg's eighth cousin twice removed he's technically a member of my family
d) That one weird cousin
e) Nice try, Mam, I'm keeping my cards close to my chest on this one

# REASONS WHY SINN FÉIN HAVE LOST SUPPORT IN THE POLLS

WITH A RECENT poll taken ahead of the upcoming EU elections suggesting Sinn Féin have suffered a dip in support, a number of political commentators in the media have provided their theories for why voters are turning away from the Republican party.

- Stockholm syndrome is a very real and serious psychological condition.
- An almost 11% drop from peak support is clearly because Simon Harris is a charisma canon, spraying his charm all over the Irish public.
- Dublin woman Tríona Hayes swore off voting for Sinn Féin after Mary Lou McDonald beat her to the last scone in her local Aldi.
- Rural independents are hoovering up the 'fecking foreigners!' vote.
- Some voters could never stomach voting for a party with IRA links hence the 5% rise in Aontú, a party led by a former Sinn Féin member.
- Willie O'Dea agreed to finally shave his moustache if people vote for Fianna Fáil.
- Sinn Féin's tiocfaidh now has 30% less ár lá than at its height.
- Turns out the public doesn't like it when TDs from the main opposition party, who claim to be able to solve the housing supply issue, keep objecting to homes being built in their own constituencies.
- Young Waterford voter Alan Tealon retracted his support after he discovered something called 'the IRA' during a routine browse of Wikipedia.
- Gerry Adams hasn't done anything meme-worthy recently.

- People like to lie when answering poll company questionnaires just to fuck with them.
- The recent solar eclipse was one giant Men In Black memory wipe and it set time itself back to 2011.
- Their long-running 'vote in the 26 counties, get 6 counties free' promotion recently ended.
- Sinn Féin's U-turn on immigration hasn't turned quickly enough.

> **Did You Know?**
> To prepare for his role as Peter Parker in *Spiderman*, actor Tom Holland stalked Tobey Maguire for two years.

15

Waterford Whispers News

## ABORTION REFORM

# SAME CROWD WHO GAVE NUNS A MATERNITY HOSPITAL PLEDGE TO GET ABORTION SERVICES REFORMS RIGHT

THE SAME government that managed to give the Sisters of Charity, most famous for being charitable with their mistreatment of women in Magdalene Laundries, a say in the running of the National Maternity Hospital is today insisting that the very same politicians can be trusted to bring through reforms to Ireland's abortion services.

> 'Nuns running a hospital, what could go wrong'

'Yes, we're dragging our heels on reforming abortion services in Ireland but honestly, you're telling me you wouldn't trust us, the "ah, nuns running a hospital, what could go wrong" guys?' said Taoiseach Simon Harris, who as Minister for Health oversaw the National Maternity Hospital debacle.

The author of the report on Ireland's abortion services, barrister Marie O'Shea, criticised a lack of action on many of the legislative recommendations contained within it.

'Ah no, that's not fair, we've only been sitting on this report and failing to act for a year. That's like a day in IPT terms,' said one coalition TD, referring to Irish Politician Time.

Government TDs were in agreement that the public should 'come back to us after 10 years of inaction' before starting to moan, referencing other long-gestating healthcare scandals such as child spinal surgery waiting lists.

'And yes, there's rogue counselling services funded by nutty US right-wing Christian groups, preying on vulnerable women and giving them misleading information on abortions, but sure what's the harm? Didn't we have the referendum a few years ago and us politicians got to pose for celebratory photos, and at the end of the day that's all that matters,' explained one TD.

### Mindlessness Tip
If things seem hard now, don't worry, that's just your inability to weather even the slightest bit of difficulty in life, you complete and utter sap.

### Community Alert
Anybody else wake up to find new blue, purple, yellow and orange bins outside their house?

Politics

## THE MIDDLE EAST

# A POLITICIAN'S GUIDE TO WRITING A PATHETIC, WEASEL-WORDED STATEMENT ON ISRAEL MURDERING AID WORKERS

IT'S A weekday ending in a 'y' so that must mean the IDF has committed at least one heinous crime that, were it committed by Russia, would see the implementation of sanctions, the expulsion of diplomats, the freezing of assets and a dozen other measures.

If you're a politician it's right about now your team of advisers should be penning a carefully worded statement that gives the impression you're condemning and criticising but also, most importantly, heavily implying Israel can just keep on doing what it is doing because there will be no consequences.

This may be your first time producing a pathetic, weasel-worded statement, so here's some tips *WWN* got from a politician because, let's face it, this won't be the last one you'll have to issue.

'Outrageous and unacceptable.' – Sounds dangerously like you're done with the brazen murder of medics, journalists, aid workers, the whole lot, which is why you need to add this little guy afterwards:

'If, after a thorough and lengthy investigation, the full facts reveal there was premeditation.' – Phew, you were nearly unequivocally stating that killing aid workers is something that should immediately carry significant cost to the perpetrators and result in Israel becoming a pariah state.

Next up: 'This cannot go on.'*

*Yes it can, and it will because your statement isn't even entertaining the idea that a country with an army that has killed more journalists than died in World War II in just six months is worthy of sanctions.

'Contravenes all laws relating to combat and engagement in a war.' – Just repeat your old friend 'must be investigated' and bingo, breaking laws doesn't have to come at the risk of you trying to do anything about it while, to an idiot, it'll sound like you're really vexed.

**Famous Quotes from 2024**
"Oh great, just what we needed, a fucking pier"
– Gazans upon hearing the news that the US plans to build a pier

'I will be bringing this up at the next sitting of [insert toothless international body which has no powers to compel Israel to do anything].' – Wow, that sounds super serious, and yet means nothing.

'This is an unforgivable act.' – Careful, you don't want to include this because that implies you might suspend arms sales to Israel or cease trading with them.

'Israel has not done enough to protect civilians.' – It sounds like a condemnation, but when it's issued nearly seven months after the beginning of an attempted genocide, the words will sound exactly as hollow and consequence-free as you want them to.

Waterford Whispers News

## ASYLUM SEEKERS

# FINE GAEL TO EXPLORE PUTTING ASYLUM SEEKERS THROUGH NEW YORK PORTAL INSTALLATION

AS PART OF their latest attempt to prove they're the 'party of law and order' after a brief sabbatical from the title for a decade plus, Fine Gael have today led a coalition government operation to clear asylum seekers from the Grand Canal.

'I'm no expert on physics but it's worth a try,' explained housing, health and governance inexpert Taoiseach Simon Harris of his new plan to see if it's possible to put international protection applicants through a new art installation, a 'virtual portal' to New York.

A call-out was made to all budding mad scientists, preferably someone with a heavy German accent and untameable hair, in a bid to get this next plan off the ground. Before The Portal is tested, Fine Gael have confirmed a number of lucrative tenders will be announced, which will allow consultancy firms to make some money.

'And hey, if this works, we can send people on trolleys in A&E through next, we ask New York for a few apartments. Boom, every crisis of our own making solved,' continued Harris, as Dublin City Council destroyed asylum seekers' tents, which will be needed again tomorrow.

Meanwhile, the CEO of one company supplying charities and the Government with tents, both large and small, has appealed for help with counting their money.

> 'And hey, if this works, we can send people on trolleys in A&E through next'

**The Year in Numbers**

As many as a worrying 3 in 5 adults over 40 do not have the basic skills required to start a TikTok trend.

**2025 Predictions**

Buildings marked for asylum seekers will continue to spontaneously combust.

Politics

**BREAKING**

# SIMON HARRIS SET TO BECOME IRELAND'S FIRST HAUNTED DOLL TAOISEACH

THE Irish haunted doll community is expected to celebrate one of their own today as Simon Harris is set to become the first haunted doll taoiseach in the history of the State.

Created from a curse over 37 years ago, the once wooden Harris was summoned by a coven of cackling witches on top of Killiney Hill using black magic and human sacrifice before being handed over to the Harris family to raise in Greystones, where he grew up to learn the dark arts of the Lord Lucifer, eventually becoming an Irish politician.

'I remember the banshee cries when he was manifested like it was yesterday,' recalls local witch Tina

Flynn, who helped sacrifice a young virgin in a bid to spawn the now

taoiseach back in October '86. 'We knew then his destiny was to become ruler of the land and the eventual anti-Christ.'

Witches at the time prophesised Harris's rise using 'a new medium', with the letters 'TT' appearing as a birth mark behind the ear of the young, haunted doll.

'From hazel wood to flesh, the beast will rise to the sound of the clock, going tick tock, tick tock,' was the witch's rhyme read out loud during the satanic sermon which spawned the young Harris child almost four decades ago.

Despite his inability to shake his wooden demeanour, the Satan-flanked Harris quickly rose up the ranks to become leader of Fine Gael last week and, if he continues on his current rapid ascent in the corridors of power, he is expected to eventually become destroyer of worlds by the time he's 50.

# 'YOU UNION JACK SHAGGERS BETTER GET USED TO SECOND CLASS CITIZEN STATUS' SAYS MICHELLE O'NEILL, IN UNIFYING MESSAGE

WITH the DUP finally getting over their two-year sulk and accepting the fact Northern Ireland will have a nationalist first minister, Sinn Féin showed true leadership when party leader Mary Lou McDonald reassured worried Unionists by immediately breaking out the champagne to celebrate a United Ireland.

'Irish unity is within touching distance,' said McDonald, deftly walking a political tightrope that, were the wrong words chosen, could lead some in Unionist communities to feel Sinn Féin's immediate priority was not improving services and infrastructure which has been neglected in recent years.

'And you Union Jack shaggers better get used to singing "Amhrán na bhFiann",' added First Minister Michelle O'Neill, in a unifying message reminiscent of Nelson Mandela.

It was the sort of shrewd comment that left the DUP no room

to deflect criticism and anger from their voters back onto an opposition who could be respected for focusing solely on improving the everyday lives of people.

'Anyone speaking English will be fined, and you'll have to dream in Irish. Schools will be supplied with only green, white and orange crayons, every day will be Bobby Storey funeral commemoration day,'

continued O'Neill, rubbishing fears Sinn Féin would forego addressing voters' concerns in favour of gloating and repeating 'United Ireland' like a monosyllabic Republican cockatoo.

'And you Alliance voters acting like you're above sectarianism can do one as well,' concluded O'Neill, winning over the last few Loyalists on the fence about this historic shift in Northern Irish politics.

19

# Waterford Whispers News

## POLLS

# NEW POLL SHOWS UNDER-35S WOULD RATHER PUT GENITALS IN BLENDER THAN VOTE FOR FF/FG

A NEW poll has revealed that Ireland's cohort of voters aged under 35 would rather place their own genitals in a blender and press the 'eviscerate' setting than consider voting for Fianna Fáil or Fine Gael in the next general election.

'I'm not saying I'd enjoy the sensation of my bollocks and mickey being pulsed into a smoothie but it won't be worse than voting this shower in again, that's for sure,' confirmed one poll taker.

The poll, which was published in today's edition of *Waterford Whispers News* revealed that the make or model of the blender or how rusty the blades are isn't important to voters in much the same way the far-fetched claims made by the current coalition partners about how their policies are delivering for young people has no bearing on their decision.

'But why? We're so hip and approachable,' said a Fine Gael spokesperson over the sounds of hip new band Coldplay playing in the background.

'If we were any more in touch with today's youth we'd be an Irish religious order,' added Fianna Fáil, who stood by their party's positive policies which have seen Ireland become a pleasuredome for property speculators.

The same poll saw Sinn Féin emerge as the most popular party in the country for the seventieth poll in a row, leading to a humbling and sobering moment for the coalition partners.

'Oh naive children, just ask your parents who you presumably still live with all about the dangers of a Sinn Féin government,' added the parties.

> **Community Alert**
> Israeli family only in the estate a wet week and they're after building an extension into the Farrelly's back garden. No planning permission, nothing.

Politics

## REFUGEES

# 'WE WANT TO GIVE THEM A REALISTIC TASTE OF IRELAND' – GOVERNMENT DEFENDS PLAN TO MAKE REFUGEES HOMELESS

A CABINET discussion on proposals to limit the offer of state-provided accommodation for Ukrainian refugees to 90 days before turfing them out onto the streets to fend for themselves was labelled 'a little bit Irish' today, *WWN* has learned.

A row over the proposals broke out among the cabinet after Minister for Equality Roderic O'Gorman suggested the changes, pointing out that as equality minister he has to treat refugees like we would treat our own people.

'We want to give them a realistic taste of Ireland,' O'Gorman stated, 'and that means just that; leaving the most vulnerable people out to rot in the elements, for charities to take care of, allowing this Government to continue failing in more important areas like health, housing and national policing.'

Raising concerns of an extra workload on his department, Housing Minister Darragh O'Brien said he was already 'fucking up as much as he possibly could for the moment', and that passing the buck and making housing Ukrainians his problem wasn't a fair ask of a housing department.

'We're already two decades behind on housing and now you want me to house even more people?' challenged O'Brien. 'I'm housed out. Christ, when's the next reshuffle? I actually hope Sinn Féin get into power so we can just watch them implode.'

With 800 new refugees arriving each week, one renegade backbencher offered a wild suggestion.

'Maybe we should just hire more special advisers to slyly imply to the public that Ireland is "full" despite the HSE alone having 400 unused vacant sites,' suggested the TD.

> 'Maybe we should just hire more special advisers to slyly imply to the public that Ireland is "full"'

**Famous Quotes from 2024**

"They're basically the Raygun of music"
– **breakdancer Raygun** on **Jedward**.

Waterford Whispers News

## UK ELECTION

# 'YOU HAVEN'T SEEN THE LAST OF US!' CONFIRM TORIES MELTING INTO PUDDLE OF TOXIC SLUDGE

FOLLOWING a humbling battering in the 4 July elections, the UK's Conservative Party have defiantly vowed that 'you haven't seen the last of us'.

Squeaking in a high-pitched voice as the effect of democracy in action reduces them from their human form into a slowly melting puddle of toxic effluent, the Tories insisted, 'we'll get our revenge'.

Clearly stating that turning the country into a basket case and isolating it on the international stage wasn't 'revenge enough', the smoking pile of putrid sludge slithered towards the nearest open manhole, beneath which it vowed to spend the next few years recuperating, and getting stronger.

'It might take a mad (and racist) scientist to turn us back into our former glory as the party of Rwanda flights, Covid contracts for mates, and MPs embroiled in embezzlement and abuse, but we shall rise from the ashes like a phoenix who lives for shitting on poor people and cutting tax for the uber-rich,' it declared.

> 'We shall rise from the ashes like a phoenix who lives for shitting on poor people'

Less electable than syphilis-powered cancer in puppies, a rare moment of candour saw the putrid curdling puddle of political poison achieve some honesty:

'Now is the time to fuse the DNA of Boris Johnson and Nigel Farage to create the first genetically modified Mega-Bastard. Wait and see, you'll all pay, pay dearly!' hissed the puddle as it slithered into the shadows.

### County Council Notices

New e-scooter lanes are to be installed in a zigzag format intersecting every car, bike and bus lane in the city to cater for riders' erratic scooting.

### The Year in Numbers

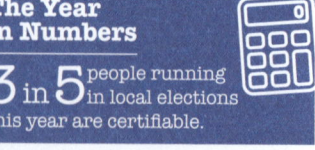

3 in 5 people running in local elections this year are certifiable.

Politics

## EUROPE

# WAS SIMON HARRIS RIGHT TO DAB DURING MEETING WITH URSULA VON DER LEYEN?

PARTAKING in his first engagements in Brussels in his role as taoiseach, Simon Harris received some criticism for trying to lead the charge in building consensus among EU nations on recognising the state of Palestine, and additional criticism for dabbing in a meeting with Ursula von der Leyen.

'Call it youthful exuberance or what have you. I knew we shouldn't have let him wolf into the Skittles on the flight over but you live and learn,' said one of Harris's 104 new PR handlers. 'I think we got away with it though as Ursula thought he was just some interrailing student who got lost and wandered into the room.'

Possibly realising that many EU leaders lack the empathy to acknowledge the horrors unfolding in Gaza, Harris appealed to their egos instead in trying to secure support.

'No cap, think about it, doing a "Dab for Gaza" trend would do big numbers on TikTok, and T-Swift's music is back on there now. We find the perfect song of hers to go over a video of me is peak rizz, and then ooh baby it's going to be raining likes,' offered Harris to a bewildered von der Leyen, who Harris then labelled 'mid at best'.

> 'We find the perfect song of hers to go over a video of me is peak rizz, and then ooh baby it's going to be raining likes'

Today Harris will meet the Spanish PM in Dublin for further discussions of recognising Palestine.

'Some people may call me a hero, and if potentially recognising Palestinian statehood a full 10 years after the bill calling for recognition passed the Oireachtas but was ignored by my party means I'm a hero, so be it,' added Harris when asked by the media about his first visit to Brussels.

**Was the Taoiseach right to dab during the meeting?**
a) It's standard TikTok diplomacy, my guy Si is playing a blinder.
b) I wouldn't worry, none of this will matter once Israel and Iran nuke us all into oblivion.

**Community Alert**

No sign of Elaine Lannigan's sisters over the Christmas, they must have had a falling out.

# WARNING

**In the event of the selfish coalition government of Ireland callously calling a general election after this book has gone to print, thus robbing Ireland's most trusted news source from including our brave coverage for our readers, please turn to page 172 to see what a Sinn Féin victory would entail.***

*According to the boffins at the Institute of Studies and Research Into Research and Studies.

# ww news

Waterford Whispers News

## LOCAL NEWS

Waterford Whispers News

## DISABILITIES

# PUBLIC GOES BACK TO IGNORING PLIGHT OF CARERS AND PEOPLE WITH DISABILITIES

AFTER having become the focal point of debate during the recent referendums amid greater visibility and temporary media interest, Ireland's carers and disabled citizens have been told not to get used to the support and advocacy as the voting public consider their bit 'done'.

'Whoa now, when I said the Government needs to do more I didn't mean that would involve me giving you lot another thought,' confirmed one person, who thought the Government should move heaven and Earth for carers in ways that didn't involve investment through taxation.

The public warned that advocacy groups and marginalised people who may be feeling the wind beneath their sails and a sense of support that has been absent for years must appreciate the public's enthusiasm has an expiry date of 'moments after casting my vote'.

'I didn't vote at all on Friday, what more do you want?' said one business owner, who spent much of last year tirelessly researching loopholes in regulations that would get him out of improving accessibility on his premises.

> 'Whoa now, when I said the Government needs to do more I didn't mean that would involve me giving you lot another thought'

### The Year in Numbers

**25%** The percentage of cloud cover in Ireland caused by teenagers' vape smoke.

'Ask me to watch a few viral TikToks on the subject, grand, that I can do. But to be part of meaningful change? C'mon, be realistic,' confirmed another person, who wouldn't have put 'ally' in her social media bios if she knew it had to mean something.

Elsewhere, one local man who went hoarse from telling people to vote no on the basis of the need for enhanced supports and access for disabled people has already reverted back to calling anyone receiving disability payments 'workshy scammers'.

Local News

RELIGION

# PARISH OUTRAGE AS PRIEST FORCED ALTAR BOY TO FORGE MASS CARDS

DOZENS of parishioners attended a protest outside Fr Murphy's residence this evening after an altar boy revealed that he was the one signing mass cards for the last three years and not the priest himself, despite people paying for the heavenly signature.

'We just feel cheated spending €5 a pop for what is essentially a blatant forgery,' local widow Peggy O'Mahony told *WWN*, echoing the sentiments of over a thousand more fraud victims.

The 13-year-old altar boy who cannot be named for legal reasons said he was forced by the priest to sign the lucrative mass cards, revealing the priest was getting them in for 'half nothing' from the Philippines and making a tidy tax-free profit believed to be into the tens of thousands of euros.

'It seems to be a sophisticated operation and a full investigation is being carried out not just here, but in other parishes as well,' said a spokesgarda investigating the fraud, which is now believed to be rife in the Roman Catholic diocese.

Mass card forgeries are the latest in a series of horrific crimes committed by the clergy, with victims now calling for a 100% redress scheme for those affected by the forgeries.

'If people who were abused by clerics or had their babies sold by nuns haven't received a red cent yet, then I certainly wouldn't be holding my breath over mass cards,' stated a government source.

An Post have since suspended selling mass cards and have urged people not to resort to purchasing them from the black market.

'It's tempting to just buy a forged card thinking no one will know the difference, but holy God will know,' An Post stated.

### Classifieds

**OLD PLASTIC BOTTLE LID COLLECTORS CLUB**

Sick of the new plastic bottle lids that you can't fully remove? Why not join a new appreciation society dedicated to old removable bottle lids that screw on and off like back in the good old days. Come view our huge collection of retro unscrewable plastic lids. Swap and share your favourite lids with other lid enthusiasts.

NOTE: new lids are strictly forbidden and owners of such may spark violence.

Town Hall, 7 p.m.

27

Waterford Whispers News

# ARSON

## RACIST ARSONISTS ASKED TO IMPROVE COMMUNICATION AND CONSULTATION

WHILE local authorities, accommodation providers, charities and the Department of Integration strive to improve their communication and consultation efforts with local communities, many see this new undertaking as an opportunity for racist arsonists to do the same.

'Some communities have rightly pointed out that our communication has been poor, and we pledge to improve on that front, so, in keeping with that spirit we similarly ask arsonists to find some other way of communicating that isn't burning a fucking building to the ground,' offered one off-the-record Department of Integration official.

'I issued a press release a day late and I got it in the ear from local councillors for my "poor communication skills", but pouring petrol all over private premises which could have had people in them at the time is hardly fuckin' Shakespeare, is it?' shared one frustrated women's shelter charity worker.

Sensible people have confirmed that letting people know months and years in advance that a derelict hotel that has sat empty for 10 years is going to be used to house asylum seekers will instantly appease and calm people to the point where they'll no longer want to burn it down.

'OK, we get it, you hate the idea of foreign migrants in your locality, but can you find a way to communicate that fact that doesn't require filling a 10-litre cylinder at a petrol pump?' shared one local politician who obviously wasn't planning on getting re-elected at this year's local elections.

> 'Pouring petrol all over private premises which could have had people in them at the time is hardly fuckin' Shakespeare, is it?'

**County Council Notices**

You talked and we listened to your points on how it's impossible to maintain a small family retail business in the city centre during these difficult times, which is why we're going to increase the rates again by another 5% this year. Thank you.

Local News

## HOMELESSNESS

# THE TOUCHING MOMENT HOMELESS IRISH MAN SHOWS HOMELESS ASYLUM SEEKER HOW TO PITCH A TENT

WHEN two worlds meet; a touching moment was captured earlier this week when an asylum seeker was snapped being taught how to pitch a tent along the Grand Canal by a native Irish man who was also homeless.

The viral encounter was praised by politicians as a real step forward in Irish and foreign national relations amid the ongoing racism being played out on city streets.

'They're so cute,' Housing Minister Darragh O'Brien commented on the scene, blatantly ignoring the 14,000 homeless figure reaching the news this week.

'This is exactly the type of scene we want to see,' Minister for Integration Roderic O'Gorman chimed in, as news that 80 asylum seekers a day flow in through the North after being denied entry in the UK.

With tent cities now becoming the norm on Dublin streets, even finding a place to erect a tent has become as hard as securing a roof over your head.

'Pretty soon the council will probably start charging us rent to sleep on the streets,' one homeless Dublin man pointed out, before being shushed by another asking him not to give the government any more ideas.

With the large influx of newcomers, the Irish homeless have been urged by the government to make their foreign counterparts feel right at home here by letting them know there is very little hope of ever getting one.

## INSURANCE

# MAN DREAMING OF BEING REAR-ENDED AFTER INSTALLING DASH CAM

A LOCAL MAN has spoken of his excitement at the prospect of being crashed into by a fellow motorist now that he has finally installed dash cams, WWN has learned.

'Them compilation videos of lads who'd be fucked on insurance claims if they didn't have dash cam footage of some prick hammering into them are just about my favourite thing in the world, and now that's a reality for me,' said Waterford man Tommy Furlong, transfixed by the feeds from his cameras mounted onto the bonnet, boot and side doors of his car.

However, Furlong has rightly concluded that there's no fun in having the dash cams if he doesn't catch someone bang to rights throwing themselves across his bonnet in a bid to secure a quick compo claim at his expense or a driver rear-ending him.

'I'm braking suddenly like no one's business these days but so far no one's bitten. Any day now, I'll have the perfect video to upload and lads on car forums will lap it up. Finally it'll be me people are saying "he would have been fucked if not for the dash" about,' Furlong said, beaming with anticipation.

A recent study revealed male drivers lose 5,000 hours of their lives every year scrolling through boring and uneventful dash cam footage on their cars in the hope of finding something worthy of clipping and uploading to YouTube.

29

Waterford Whispers News

## SOCIAL MEDIA

# IT'S 1,200 YEARS SINCE THE VIKINGS INVADED AND IRISH PEOPLE ARE SHARING THEIR MEMORIES ON SOCIAL MEDIA

THERE'S no minor or major historical event or cultural moment that can't be given the nostalgia treatment on social media, and the Viking invasion of Ireland is no different as social media users proved today, with many sharing their fond recollections of the moment 1,200 years ago to the day the Vikings first landed in Waterford.

'Jesus, where does the time go? 1,200 years already? Remember the state they left the place in with their pillaging like it was yesterday,' recalled one misty-eyed X user.

**'Who's the eejit with the horns on their helmet'**

'Can remember thinking, "who's the eejit with the horns on their helmet, gas" – so random, like why Ireland bro?' chimed one TikTok user.

'Pricks introduced the longboat to Ireland, importing their culture! Ireland went to the dogs the day they rowed in,' added a Facebook user.

'It was hard enough being a rural bachelor with a face like a baked potato before those gorgeous fuckers arrived, I haven't got the ride since,' shared one Instagram user.

'And I thought Dublin stag dos were bad but these blonde pricks had no manners, shite tippers too,' one barman shared on X.

'They ruined Christmas 'round my uncle's that year. Twins my aunt had, blonder than a bottle of Clairol Nice'n Easy Blonde they were. Can still see her face trying to justify calling them Odin and Loki as well. Uncle was never the same, got lost in the mead after that,' another X user shared.

**Famous Quotes from 2024**

"Esto es no bueno"
– Mexican Sinaloa Cartel, on the seizure of €34m of their crystal meth in Cork

Local News

# EDUCATION

# WHY PEOPLE WHO WENT TO SAME-SEX SCHOOLS THINK THEY GOT THE BEST EDUCATION

AS DEBATE about the merits of single-sex schools rears its head once more, *WWN* spoke to a number of Irish people to find out their experiences attending such schools to gauge the positive experiences and showcase that while some find it archaic, single-sex schooling has a place in the future of the Irish education system.

'I'm lucky I went to a single-sex school, otherwise I'd only been distracted and that would have stopped all chance of me securing that D3 in foundation level Irish.'
– David, Waterford

'As the only femme lesbian in school I cleaned up!'
– Sarah, Cork

'I feel sorry for lads that went to a mixed school, they had to endure the physical bullying from male students AND the psychological warfare from female students on top of that? Awful.'
– Ryan, Wicklow

'Had I gone to a mixed school I would never have discovered the joy that is having panic attacks when talking to the opposite sex.'
– Sean, Dublin

'As a parent now myself I think it's important to make sure your children have the same insulated upbringing that helped form some of your most debilitating flaws, it's good to be able to pass on these things.'
– Shauna, Meath

'Thanks to the school I was placed in, I never had to interact with a man, and to this day I still haven't met one.'
– Aoife, Galway

### The Year in Numbers
## 132,640
The record number of times 'why won't this feckin' yoke work?' was uttered in Ireland in 2024, thanks to the Deposit Return Scheme.

'Being in a single-sex school would have been made much more problematic if Irish schools got their sex-ed from elderly virgins who dressed up as wizards but thankfully that wasn't the case.'
– Liam, Sligo

'Mixed in with girls? Ha, let me tell you something, people say single-sex schools are bad but by being in one without those thieving, lying, two-faced bitches I was much better off.'
– Kevin, Wexford

## Waterford Whispers News

### EXCLUSIVE

# RIPPED ENOCH BURKE IN GYM ALL DAY LEADING RELIGIOUS PRISON GANG

PRISON sources have revealed today that Enoch 'The Knocker' Burke is settling into prison life quite well. He has doubled his body mass in just 275 days and is now leader of an entire Mountjoy Prison wing after converting dozens of inmates to 'whatever batshit branch of Christianity he's a part of'.

Still receiving his teacher's salary while inside despite a permanent injunction restraining him from attending the school he was barred from, The Knocker Burke's fortune has given him leverage over his fellow prisoners, putting down contracts on non-believers and targeting all forms of homosexuality in the prison.

'He'd sometimes lay gay traps like bars of soap in the showers to see who'd "try it",' an anonymous prison source told WWN, and who admitted to being scared for their life.

'He has a strict no pronoun rule across D wing and will condemn any of his followers to hell for even saying the word "they",' the source added. 'Have you any idea how hard it is not to use the word "they" in everyday life? It's just a fucking word.'

Burke stated at a court hearing yesterday that he has spent almost a year behind bars because he was being punished for his opposition to 'transgenderism' and his refusal to comply with a direction from the school to address a teenage student by a different pronoun.

'You're in prison because you refuse to stop creeping around the school you've been fired from, for not paying huge fines and for also being a little prick in court,' the exhausted judge concluded.

> **'He'd sometimes lay gay traps like bars of soap in the showers'**

### 2025 Predictions

After turning Argentina's economic fortunes around, President Javier Milei is voted in as Limerick mayor.

Local News

## LEITRIM

# SUSPICIONS RAISED AS NO ONE HAS EVER MET SOMEONE FROM LEITRIM

APPEALS HAVE been made for people from Leitrim to come forward and make themselves known after a worrying survey revealed no one has ever met someone from the alleged county, WWN can reveal.

'We urge anyone from Leitrim to raise your hands and provide proof, we don't want another nonsense prank like when people claimed to be from "Carlow", no time wasters please,' insisted a CSO worker tasked with incorporating Leitrim-based statistics into the national records.

It has long been claimed Leitrim is a CIA PsyOp, launched by the CIA as it wanted to see if, on a small scale at first, a population could be tricked into believing something so obviously fabricated. Once Ireland was fooled, that was their go-ahead to run with the 'Saddam had nukes' story.

However, in the years that followed suspicions grew about Leitrim people on account of no one famous coming from the county, not even a Fair City actor or Instagram influencer.

The GAA have confirmed that after searching their own records they found someone retroactively tampered with the records and used Tipp-Ex to claim the county won the 1994 Connacht championship.

'We ask the public to keep an eye out too, we've no idea what Leitrim folk look like but we imagine it's not too far off some Bigfoot-looking sort,' added the CSO official.

**Mindlessness Tip**

3 a.m. is the best time to wake up and worry about everything before finally drifting off to sleep 5 minutes before your work alarm is due to go off.

# NEW RED LIGHT CAMERAS WON'T WORK ON JUDGES, POLITICIANS, OFF-DUTY GUARDS OR GAA PLAYERS

**County Council Notices**

Oh don't let the name fool you, the County Council will continue to just focus on city issues and keep those rural issues for the next general election.

A CHILL may have travelled down the spine of every responsible driver across Ireland who routinely breaks red lights when Minister for Transport Eamon Ryan confirmed red light cameras which issue automatic fines will be installed nationwide next year. However, much-needed reassurances have been given to a number of people.

'As is customary with road traffic offences that carry penalty points and fines, the usual cohort of important people will be exempt,' confirmed a government spokesperson for half-arsed implementation of regulations.

It was feared that such brazen attempts to punish the perfectly 'grand' variety of irresponsible driving habits could unintentionally affect people who are too important to be treated like other members of the public.

'I nearly dropped my phone I was using to live-stream on TikTok when I heard the news as I was bombing down the M7,' confirmed one Irish judge, who was relieved to have the traditional guarantee that a nod and wink arrangement will be in place for certain groups.

While the red light cameras will operate as normal for regular drivers, the nation's judges, politicians, off-duty guards and GAA players will have their licence plates fitted with a QR code the red light cameras will automatically recognise.

'And yeah, up pops "Not A Pleb" and then we don't issue the fine,' confirmed one system operator, 'but don't worry if the QR code yoke doesn't work, the camera software has been trained on thousands of hours of garda traffic stops so it's automatically able to register that air of self-importance and arrogance that gets you a let-off.'

33

Waterford Whispers News

## EDUCATION

# TRINITY STUDENTS FINED €214,000 FOR PAYING ATTENTION IN POLITICS LECTURES

**Community Alert**
Unvetted male! Unvetted male! Unvetted male! Unvetted male! Wait, false alarm, it's just my Kieran.

TRINITY COLLEGE has been left with no choice but to issue a hefty €214,000 fine to the college's Student Union after members held a number of disruptive tourist income-sapping protests, sparked in part by the contents of lectures detailing the inequality which serves as the foundations for western economies.

'I always said Sally Rooney and her little romcommunist books would lead to this!' raged a TCD spokesperson, who insisted students weren't supposed to take sociology, economics and politics lectures so literally.

'If we had suspected offering degrees that could potentially educate people on social inequality and the sins of capitalism we'd never have allowed it,' added the spokesperson, who regretted the fact that some students insisted on learning about the intricacies of international diplomacy and the rules that govern it, and calling for them to be enforced.

In a bid to avoid a repeat of students protesting the fact TCD invests in UN-blacklisted Israeli firms, PhD student pay, or the rise in the cost of campus accommodation, it has been rumoured the university's provost might consider suspending degrees that could lead to students questioning the world around them.

'Philosophy lectures can continue as normal because none of that means anything,' clarified a spokesperson.

Meanwhile, in a *WWN* yes-or-no poll asking if the public backed student protests over accommodation costs, 100% of respondents said 'typical naive students, wait until they're in the real world and need to earn, not just mooch around doing nothing, never worked a day in their lives, and what's that haircut about? Good luck being taken seriously with that dangly little earring, and him a fella, Jesus the world has gone to the dogs. Softer than an arse made of feathers on a velvet cushion! Parents rich as anything too, I'd say. The dogs! Gone to the dogs!'

Local News

## FUNDRAISERS

# 'ANY FREE TICKETS?' MAN ASKS FRIEND ORGANISING FUNDRAISER EVENT

LIKE clockwork, local man Damien Lyons has slid into the DMs of friend and events organiser Mary Holden to see if there are any free tickets to the charity fundraising event she's organising as he 'absolutely loves' the acts she has booked.

Mere seconds after she posted the event online, freeloader Lyons opened with his usual 'where do I get tickets for this?' line, followed quickly with him just blatantly asking for free passes.

'Myself and Linda haven't had a night out in ages,' said Lyons, emotionally blackmailing his friend, who only saw the pair hammered last Saturday at a free wine tasting in the local off-licence. 'We don't have the kids that night either. Looks like it will be great craic. Fair play for organising it.'

Despite the fact the event clearly states all proceeds will go towards brain surgery for a child suffering from cancer, Lyons toyed with the idea of inviting his friends in the hopes of giving back.

'I can ask Terry and June too if you have two more spare, they're minted and will definitely throw a few quid on the raffle,' Lyons added to his thread, not intending to contribute anything himself as showing his face and providing moral support for his friend Mary is 'charity enough'.

'Fuck off, Damien, this is a charity gig; if you want to go buy some fucking tickets then here's the link – I'm up to me hoop here,' Holden replied, now sick of his shit.

'Actually, no worries, Mary, just remembered Linda has a hair appointment – totally forgot – catch you soon for a coffee though, my shout,' Lyons promised, knowing full well he only contacts friends when he needs something.

> 'Fuck off, Damien, this is a charity gig; if you want to go buy some fucking tickets then here's the link'

### Famous Quotes from 2024

"Where's the brakes on this thing?"
– **Captain of the** *Dali* **container ship before hitting Francis Scott Key Bridge**

Waterford Whispers News

## ADVICE COLUMN

# ASK ANNE: 'I MURDERED MY NEIGHBOUR'S FAMILY AND NOW SHE'S BADMOUTHING ME IN THE RESIDENTS GROUP CHAT'

**OUR RESIDENT advice columnist Anne Trope helps readers with their dilemmas.**

Dear Anne,
I am subject to an ill-tempered and irrational vendetta from an unreasonable neighbour and it's affecting my reputation among my neighbours.

Some years ago I murdered my neighbour's entire family. Now that I have returned home after some time away (prison, for the murders) my neighbour is claiming to the rest of our estate in a group chat that I'm some kind of monster. She is the group admin and I can't even gain access to defend myself.

For context, she's not even mentioning the full context. The reason I murdered her husband and children is because they were seriously annoying. To say she's being uncivil is putting it mildly, she's the Dublin riots of people.

The badmouthing is hurtful and causing me great pain and anguish, the sort you'd normally associate with something as severe as losing a loved one.

All appeals for her to cease her gossip spreading and insinuations about my character have so far failed. What can I do?

*In all my time doing this advice column I have never come across something so tone deaf and self-centred. So, because you murdered her family, she gets to slag you off to the neighbours? She sounds like a nasty piece of work. Sadly, some people are just bitter and don't like to see people thriving.*

*The hurt and pain in your letter is clear for all to see; oftentimes cruel people such as your neighbour have no appreciation of the hurt they cause.*

*My suggestion is if you can gain access to the group chat, posing as a different resident perhaps, you could write a message in support of yourself. Off the top of my head maybe say something like, 'is this what your annoying-as-fuck husband and kids would want you to be doing? In their memory, wind your neck in and stop your trash talk or who knows, maybe you'll be joining them sooner than you think.'*

*The tone of this message clearly indicates that bitterness and negativity can take years off someone's life and lead to increased blood pressure and a possible heart attack. Your helpful message will clearly be read as concern for your neighbour's health and will help her to make a breakthrough herself and change her bad mouthing ways.*

Local News

## RELIGION

# PILGRIMS FLOCK TO DEFECATING STATUE OF VIRGIN MARY

WHILE the Vatican has spent weeks trying to bury the story, pilgrims from around the world keep flocking to a rural Irish village to gaze in wonder at an unfolding miracle.

'Look, there, I see it, a liquid message straight from her unmentionable,' cried out one pilgrim who had travelled all the way from Bolivia, as the statue of the Virgin Mary at a grotto in Ballinferet began weeping from its posterior.

'Could it be a sign from God that the Church needs to be weaned out of the body with a spiritual laxative? I can't say,' local priest Fr Peter O'Neill told *WWN*, in what is the first official comment from a member of the clergy since the miraculous defecating started in October last year.

> 'I heard a low rumbling, which turned out to be the statue's bowels'

It didn't take long for hawkers to start selling trinkets and memorabilia depicting the miracle, with a replica statue with a button that triggers defecating priced at €25.

The first person to report seeing the statue take a dump was local woman Fidelma Rodgers and she spoke to *WWN* of the amazing interaction.

'I asked Mary for a sign that everything would be right with the world and then I heard a low rumbling, which turned out to be the statue's bowels and next thing I'm getting awful brown backsplash and this wave of number two flooded out. Why I've been blessed in such a way I don't know but I'm never showering again,' Rodgers said, who credits the incident with reigniting her dormant faith.

### County Council Notices

We can confirm the whole town is to become Ireland's first safe injection zone as part of a trial.

### 2025 Predictions

Immigration will remain the most talked-about subject in the country by a media ignoring the public's top concerns such as housing, health and childcare.

## Waterford Whispers News

### MANNERS
# DUBLIN MOTHER TO MODERATE PORTAL WITH WOODEN SPOON

IN A bid to put manners on misbehaving people at the controversial new art installation, Dublin mother Geraldine Ryan has been employed to man The Portal with a wooden spoon, *WWN* has learned.

The mother of nine will make sure no one dares perform lewd acts or brandish images of terror attacks on their phones as the people from New York watch on.

'I'll redden their fucking holes,' the 43-year-old inner city resident warned as she cleaned the portal's screen, something she isn't being requested to do but will do anyway due to 'people's grubby paws'. 'I had to put three young lads over me knee already this mornin', don't make you be the fourth,' she now shouted at a retreating youth in a Canada Goose jacket.

> **'I had to put three young lads over me knee already this mornin''**

A series of incidents involving 'inappropriate behaviour' prompted a suspension of the live stream from 10 p.m. Dublin time last night, leading to a curfew being implemented on the art installation's live feed.

'I've got the beds to change and then make the lads lunch so I can't stay on past 8 p.m.,' Mrs Ryan said, explaining why she couldn't guarantee 24/7 behaviour at the site, 'but let me tell everyone this, if someone dares try any of that auld shit when my back is turned, I'll come down on them like a tonne of bricks.'

### Mindlessness Tip
Over 800 million people suffer from hunger around the world, but yeah sure that 5-minute wait for your morning coffee was really something.

### Classifieds

**PATRIOT FOREST MEET**

Attention all ginger-bearded, skin-headed white male patriots. I'm organising a meet in the local Coillte woods on dole day at 6 p.m. for all the die-hard Irish patriots out there who are just sick of what's going on at the moment. Please wear camo combats and bring as many Irish flags as you can to show your support in a social media picture that I'll take for my Telegram channel Irish Bear. I'll be the one holding the smartphone gimbal and microphone with no friends. BYOC
Cáthál

Local News

**ON THIS DAY**

# Waterford Whispers News

VOL 3, 5612268     IRELAND, WEDNESDAY, MAY 8, 2024     €2.50

## Genocide Livestreamed On Internet To Indifference Of World

THE ONGOING starvation and indiscriminate murder of Palestinians in Gaza has continued unabated today to much shoulder shrugging, *WWN* can report.

In what historians of the future will surely pinpoint as a nadir for the Western 'rules-based order' and an end to any boasts of the West being a moral authority over the rest of the world, 8 May 2024 scrolled by to much indifference, despite humanity being at the unique point in history at which Gazans are able to document their slow unceasing eradication by the IDF online at every turn.

'Never have we had as much evidence, freely available to every living human to bear witness to, and had such a potent mix of apathy,' remarked one person, who believed themselves to be in the throes of insanity due to observing the horrors emanating from Gaza while simultaneously listening to excitable conversation between coworkers regarding the latest must-watch true crime documentaries.

Various governments around the world issued the usual statements, which neither had material effect nor threatened any sanctions against Benjamin Netanyahu's war crime-committing government. Despite the IDF themselves uploading footage of their tanks launching missiles at tents, among other indefensible acts, elected politicians in the EU and America made sure to say things like, 'we respect Israel's right to defend itself'.

'We're living through history,' offered another person, discussing yet another embarrassing Champion's League exit for PSG.

Elsewhere, the livestreaming continued.

**DEFENCE**

## IRELAND PLACE INFLATABLE WAR SHIPS IN WATERS TO WARD OFF RUSSIAN SUBMARINES

Several inflatable swimming pool toy manufacturers secured contracts for making inflatable naval vessels which look eerily like vessels actually capable of guarding and monitoring the activities of a foreign navy, such as that of Russia.

'We ordered the inflatable submarines but they just won't stay under water, we're still trying to figure out the problem there,' said the head of procurement at the Department of Defence.

'We should be good as long no one drops a Swiss army knife on these bad boys,' said Minister of Defence Simon Coveney, shortly before striking the ceremonial bottle of Champagne against the inflatable, only for it to come back and strike him in the face.

The first of the vessels, the LÉ *Johnny Logan*, is now fully operational and should serve as a major deterrent to Russian submarines as well as end all talk of a recruitment and funding crisis in the Irish Defence Forces.

Elsewhere, in an EU attempt to plug the gap in military aid to Ukraine in the wake of US Republicans holding US funding hostage, Europe's leaders have sent a clear message that they won't entertain similarly pro-Putin stances by releasing €10bn in blocked funding to Hungary's pro-Putin prime minister Viktor Orbán.

39

Waterford Whispers News

# DRINKING

# 10-YEAR-OLD'S COMEDOWN FROM PRIME PREPARING HIM FOR FUTURE DRUG USE

PUMPING HIMSELF full of enough Prime to give a herd of elephants a collective heart attack, 10-year-old Cian Shotten is unwittingly helping himself prepare for any possible future drug use he may partake in.

'I feel like I could complete Fortnite and Minecraft at the same

**'I feel like I could complete Fortnite and Minecraft at the same time!'**

time!' screamed Cian, somehow finding the required velocity to run vertically up the walls, much to the dismay of his mother Carol.

The bitter, sudden and gloom-laden comedown that abruptly hit Cian like a train carrying 47,000 tonnes of industrial-strength depression has been seen as a useful educational tool.

'Well, at least he'll be prepared for his rave days in college,' reasoned Carol, now running her fingers through her son's hair and reassuring him that no, everyone doesn't hate him and the Government aren't spying on him, he's just coming down off Prime.

### Famous Quotes from 2024

"The things I've seen, oh God the things I've seen"
- **Dublin portal**

While concerns over the energy drink part owned by 'Them Two YouTube Eejits' have cited the fact that corpses have been known to reanimate after being fed a spoonful of Prime, GPs have suggested that there has been an overreaction by some parents.

'Just do what I do with my Prime-drinking child and shoot them with a tranquiliser dart,' advised one GP, while one local drug dealer said he would never let anyone put that filth in his body.

### Mindlessness Tip
Get out into the fresh air, walk to the ocean, see people in their dryrobes and say, 'thank God I'm not one of those dryrobe pricks.'

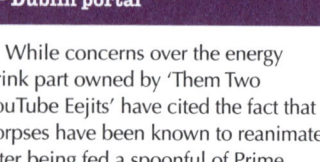

Local News

**FAMILY**

# PARENTS FONDLY REMEMBER HOW MUCH THEY LOVED SON BEFORE HE MOVED BACK IN

A DUBLIN couple have spoken movingly for the first time about how much they adored their dearly beloved son Conor before the 33-year-old tragically moved back home in a bid to save for a deposit.

'Conor was the light of my life,' confirmed mother Therese Morton, dabbing her wet eyes with a tissue.

'Ah Conor was … was? Gah, it's so strange saying it in the past tense but y'know he's a complete wreck the head now he's back in the house and regressing to his lazy teenage self,' added the man's distraught father, Graham.

Having enjoyed what they said was a 'lovely if short-lived' time when Conor lived on the other side of the city and only visited occasionally, the homeowners say once-treasured aspects of his personality have become unbearable now he spends all his time in the house.

'He was always value for money when having an amusing rant about work but not every fecking evening,' offered Therese, who mourns the son she once had when he was seldom seen and just threw her the odd text every now and then.

The pair criticised the lack of supports for parents dealing with having their adult children back in the house.

'Sometimes I walk into the sitting room and get the most awful shock when I see him scratching his hole on the couch and in command of the TV remote – for a brief moment I'd forgot he hadn't fucked off out the house. Where's the therapy supports for this sort of grief?' added Therese, shoveling Conor's rancid boxers into the washing machine.

**2025 Predictions**
Rafah can't help but take offence as it is twinned with Clonmel.

**The Year in Numbers**

17 The number of positive thoughts people not from Cork have had about Cork so far this decade.

Waterford Whispers News

## CONGRATULATIONS

# SPLIT CONDOM CELEBRATES 18TH BIRTHDAY

A SPLIT condom is the centre of attention today as it celebrates its 18th birthday, surrounded by friends and family.

'God, time flies,' confirmed mother Deirdre Kelly, who can't believe it's been about 18 years and 4 months since she beat her husband Mark Kelly around the head with her purse when she discovered she was pregnant.

'I wasn't sure at the time when I took it off after a quickie, it was my birthday I think but I suspected it had a rip in it, and judging by our Sean blowing out his candles here, it has been confirmed beyond all doubt that the condom definitely split,' explained Mark.

Aunts, uncles and grandparents have been praised for their ability not to bring up the fact they all have distinct memories of Deirdre and Mark explicitly stating, 'I don't know how we're going to afford another one' and 'fuck sake'.

> **'Judging by our Sean blowing out his candles here, it has been confirmed beyond all doubt that the condom definitely split'**

'For he's a jolly good fellow,' tunelessly sang the split condom's closest and most beloved people, raising an alcoholic drink to signify the condom was now old enough to legally drink.

'Look at it there, looks so different from when we first threw it in the bin in the bathroom,' said Deirdre and Mark as they embraced and became misty eyed.

### Did You Know?
It only took Stardust families 43 years of constant and exhausting campaigning to get justice in Ireland.

### Famous Quotes from 2024
"Christ above, even I don't like our music as much as you Irish freaks"
– Chris Martin on playing Croke Park for four nights

## DEATH

# FUNERAL HEARS GRANNY WAS SOME GOER IN HER DAY

THE small Waterford village of Grangemartin gathered this morning to bid farewell to local woman Marian Brady, a grandmother to 14 children, who were all helped in their mourning by hearing what a passionate knob polisher their grandmother was back in the day.

In a loving eulogy, her husband John spoke movingly of the fact that 'there wasn't a mickey within five miles she couldn't draw from memory' and that weeks would go by without John hearing from her when she 'was off on one of her sexcapades'.

'If it wasn't a swingers party it was a couple of German tourists passing through town, and that's not all they passed through if you catch my drift,' John said of the 81-year-old, adding that his wife was the finest and most prolific pervert he had the pleasure of knowing, and that her skills were unmatched.

'She was more than a grandmother, a mother, a teacher – although she was proud of those things – she was also a demon in the sack.'

The warm sentiments relayed by her husband were then echoed by Marian's former work colleagues, neighbours, bridge club members and random strangers who had had the pleasure of experiencing her ferocious appetite for sex and drugs.

'Chem sex? Hadn't heard of it until Marian was bored one night home alone and propositioned myself and my wife. That was the best night of my life,' confirmed neighbours Terry and Mary Langford, pointing out how strange her passing was as they only saw her naked in the bed last week.

# 'FORWARDED MANY TIMES' SAYS LADS' WHATSAPP MESSAGE CONTAINING CONTENT SO VILE IT'LL ALTER YOUR BRAIN'S CHEMISTRY FOREVER

THE HARBINGER of doom 'forwarded many times' has made itself known again in a WhatsApp group entitled 'De Mad Cuntz', and brings with it an almost 100% guarantee that the attached video will contain some of the most heinous and disturbing imagery ever committed to the internet.

'Aw fuck, no' sighed member of the group Brian Corless as fellow member David 'Diggs' Dignam sent in his fifth video of the day, each one more depraved than the last, all accompanied by a flurry of crying laughing emojis irrespective of whether they involve an Indian man beheading himself after sticking his head out the window of a moving train, a woman having sex with a horse or an ISIS terrorist blowing himself up with a grenade.

'Deep breaths, Brian,' Corless coached himself, summoning either the strength to watch the video or the good sense to immediately delete it without viewing it.

'This is the shit the CIA would use in the 80s to break a man's spirit but we're here in 2024 voluntarily watching them for shits and giggles?' added Corless, who, judging by the thumbnail on a fresh video forwarded into the group, believed this was an underground Russian dog-fighting ring compilation.

Psychologists seeking to understand what being a member of a lads' WhatsApp group can do to the human mind quit en masse within minutes of coming into contact with a video so heavy on graphic content Jeffrey Dahmer might even send in an 'ah lads that's not on' message into the group.

Elsewhere, it has emerged similar concerns surround 'forwarded many times' messages sent by mothers in family chat groups which frequently warn against scams involving people stealing your legs as you sleep if you open a video called 'SatanChallenge'.

43

Waterford Whispers News

## HEALTH

# NEW LOTTO DRAW GIVES WINNER CHANCE OF REGISTERING WITH A GP

THE IRISH national lottery has unveiled another new weekly draw with a lucrative prize that will make you the envy of everyone, *WWN* can report.

At a glitzy launch heralding the eye-watering lotto game, the new Finding A GP grand prize will see one lucky winner getting through to a GP receptionist and successfully registering with a doctor and booking an appointment.

'We're already seeing record levels of ticket sales,' said one lotto official of the tickets, which retail at €4.

More precious than gold, the Finding A GP prize will be highly sought after by anyone moving to a new area only to find out there's some octogenarian GP operating in a town of 2,000 people who has repeatedly delayed their retirement because there was no one to replace them.

Currently the odds of getting a GP at first inquiry is lower than winning

**Community Alert**

Could the couple in number 14 open their windows, we can barely make out what you two are arguing over.

the Euromillions on the same day Margot Robbie slides into your DMs.

'Fuck it, I'm cursing myself for playing the normal lotto,' said one recent millionaire, who despite her winnings has been repeatedly told by her GP's receptionist, who has the telephone manner of a prison guard turned serial killer, that there are no appointments available.

However, not everyone is happy with the news of the new draw.

'The small print says the winner is still only allowed a 15-minute consultation and if they bring up more than one ailment they will be fired into the sun,' shared one lotto player.

Local News

**EXCLUSIVE**

# MOTHER'S DYING WISH IS TO ATTEND 'PLEASURE BOYS' TOUR

DESPITE a recent and devastating terminal diagnosis, 69-year-old Waterford mother Triona Hanley is not wasting time on tears, focusing instead on ticking a number of items off her bucket list.

'Mam, what do you mean terminal!?' Hanley's son Martin asked as the mother of four explained that she doesn't care if they've finished their Irish tour, her dying wish is for her family to get her a front row seat of a Pleasure Boys XXL show.

'Oh God, Mam, c'mere, you poor thing,' added Hanley's eldest daughter Deirdre, as her mother aggressively shunned her emotional advances in favour of grabbing her phone and sending the Pleasure Boys tour dates into the family WhatsApp.

Outlining how it mattered little to her the cost, Hanley said if her children loved her they would empty her grandchildren's Credit Union accounts and book her flights, accommodation and tickets.

> 'I don't care if you have to pay extra so I'm the one getting a mickey the size of the M50 slapped about my face'

'I don't care if you have to pay extra so I'm the one getting a mickey the size of the M50 slapped about my face, make it happen, I'm your mother and I'm dying … dying to be tossed around by these oiled-up gods,' continued Hanley, keen to stress she'd prefer the buff lad who had an arse on him like two oranges in a hanky.

Hovering over the online ticket checkout on the website, Hanley's children made sure to ask their mother if she really wanted the premium 'get so dick-dizzy and cock-struck that you'll scandalise your whole family and be the talk of the town' package.

'Get me whatever ticket will result in the priest refusing to bury me in the family plot,' concluded Hanley.

---

**Mindlessness Tip**

New Year's resolutions can put too much pressure on people, so pick something easy like 'occasionally wearing something other than a comfy tracksuit'.

---

**The Year in Numbers**

**22,308**

The number of 'do we have too many immigrants?' polls Irish media ran in the last month.

Waterford Whispers News

**MOTORING**

# DUBLIN MAN MORTIFIED AFTER FILLING JEEP UP WITH NORMAL DIESEL INSTEAD OF PREMIUM

RANGE Rover Sport owner James Keegan has voiced his disgust at an unnamed fuel station today for refusing to extract diesel from his tank after he mistakenly filled it with normal diesel instead of premium.

Threatening to take the franchise station to court, Keegan claimed he's mortified driving around on the cheap yellow label fuel, hoping no one will notice his mistake.

**2025 Predictions**

The Irish Army unveils a prototype for rocket-mounted llamas.

'Like, the premium and normal pumps are almost identical. Plus being right beside each other doesn't help matters, either, ja know?' the 37-year-old Killiney man, who actually lives in Ballybrack, explained his predicament.

Wearing a baseball hat and glasses to hide his shame, Keegan contemplated trading in his 242 reg SUV for a newer version but was told there were no 243 regs and that he'd have to wait until the new year.

> 'There's no way I'm driving up in this; they'll smell the culchie fumes a mile away'

'The bloody Rover is ruined now,' he added mid-tantrum. 'I was meant to meet the guys later at the K, there's no way I'm driving up in this; they'll smell the culchie fumes a mile away.'

Despite extortionate fuel prices over the past two years, certain stations continue to flaunt premium diesel at motorists, defending the option by stating, 'there's always someone out there with notions'.

## Local News

### TAX

# LOCAL WOMAN VOWS TO REMAIN STAUNCH SOCIALIST UNTIL SALARY HITS 40% TAX BRACKET

**Did You Know?**
In Ireland, 'you're some fucking cunt altogether' is a term of endearment.

A VOCAL proponent of socialist values and the need for the rich profiteers and high-wealth individuals to be taxed in order to fund a social safety net and public infrastructure has vowed to completely lose her shit the day she reaches the 40% threshold.

Siofra Hughes (24) has maintained she will play her part in the inevitable worker uprising that can and will reshape Irish society for the better, bringing an end to flagrant materialism and short-sighted decisions that always favour the rich. However, Hughes has inserted a rather important caveat into her unwavering belief in the redistribution of wealth.

'Paying your proportionate amount of tax is all part of the social contract, solidarity with your neighbour and the worker, and this is something I'll firmly believe right up until that first payslip where I enter the highest bracket USC,' Hughes offered.

The oppressive structures of capitalism are too forceful and too great for Hughes to ignore while still in her entry-level position in the engineering firm she began working for last year, but the Cork woman conceded that that all goes out the window when she finally gets enough money for several big holidays a year, nicer clothes and a new car.

'I think it was Marx or Engels who first said, "bitch better have my money" and I really do believe that in respect of having your pay packet plundered by the thieving State to the tune of 40 cent on the euro; it's a fucking travesty, never mind the marginal tax rate, all while the scroungers get everything for free paid for by the likes of me,' confirmed committed egalitarian Hughes after a salary review placed her in the 40% income tax bracket.

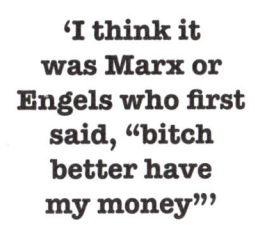

> 'I think it was Marx or Engels who first said, "bitch better have my money"'

**County Council Notices**
The River Suir will be drained at 3 p.m. today to allow for local supermarkets to reclaim their shopping trolleys.

47

Waterford Whispers News

## THE MIDDLE EAST

# IRISHMAN'S INHERITED FAMINE TRAUMA NOT STRONG ENOUGH TO TAKE INTEREST IN STARVING PALESTINIANS

NEVER missing an opportunity to berate an ignorant British person over the aggravating role of their homeland in the deliberate starving of his ancestors in Ireland, local man Colm O'Farron's inherited Famine-era trauma isn't proving strong enough to result in even a passing interest in the unfolding famine in Gaza.

'Sure, as I've been telling it for all these years half my family either died or fled for America, awful it was. Genocide it was, and the Brits still won't admit it today,' O'Farron has said over the years, in at least 1,238 displays of keenly observed performative anger.

However, the haunted pleading of his starving ancestors has remained largely dormant as he quickly scrolls past any mention of Gazans' acute food insecurity on his social media feeds.

'You would think news reports about desperate starving people eating grass and drinking polluted water would strike a chord with me, given how much I lecture people after a few pints about the impact the Famine has had on centuries of Irish art, poetry, music and story, but you'd be wrong,' said O'Farron, scrolling effortlessly past any social media posts on Gaza.

A key cornerstone to the Irish identity he has shared with any person he has ever met while travelling abroad, the Waterford man's sense of simmering fury at such injustices has so far shown no risk of boiling over when it comes to a famine he is actually alive and present for.

'I've sort of tuned it out, man, but it's mad stuff, I guess, dunno. Anyway, d'ya mind,' O'Farron said to a co-worker who brought up the subject, before allowing himself to get back to picking his fantasy football team for the weekend.

> **'I've sort of tuned it out, man, but it's mad stuff, I guess'**

## Local News

### EXCLUSIVE
# COUNCIL GONNA WAIT FOR A FEW FATALITIES FIRST BEFORE FIXING DANGEROUS JUNCTION

NOT satisfied that the unusually high number of accidents is enough to warrant immediate action to address a notorious black spot junction, the local county council has confirmed it will wait for a few fatalities first before fixing anything.

'Oh no, we've tons of money, it's just a lot of paperwork, you know?' explained a source inside Town Hall, ignoring several phones ringing in the background. 'We consistently underspent our budgets over the years but as soon as a general election is close or a few road deaths hit the news and spark some protests from people then we'll be right on it.'

Regularly in the local radio and news for accidents that disrupt traffic, the future family-member killer is expected to be used in political social media posts once sorted, with sitting councillors and politicians ready to announce how 'delighted' they are to take credit for the works, which should have been done pre-fatalities.

'It's always better fixing a poorly planned junction that has killed rather than one that hasn't killed yet,' says local councillor Terry Davis, in an attempt to explain the logic.

'Best wait for a couple of road deaths to really give my future social media announcement about fixing the junction some oomph,' he continued. 'It's the Irish way.'

#### Mindlessness Tip
Driving 20kmph under the speed limit is a great way to transfer all your negativity to the drivers stuck behind you.

---

# GOOD NEWS AS GREENWAY PLANNED BETWEEN YOUR FRONT DOOR AND LOCAL PUB

FINALLY, some good news is coming your way as the local county council has announced funding to develop an urban greenway from your front door all the way to your local pub, *WWN* can confirm.

With an expected completion date of next week, you will now be able to avail of the motor-propelled vehicle-free pathway while enjoying all the wondrous nature along the new sustainable route.

'You can get on your bike and cycle to the pub and back, sure no one will be stopping anyone drunk on a bike or e-scooter anyway,' a spokesman for the new project outside your home said today as a local councillor you've never heard of turned the sod and took credit for the entire plan.

Built just for you, the new greenway is expected to generate thousands of euros for your local pub as you basically can't go anywhere else now due to the new development.

'Yeah, it's a fairly one-way system but where else would you want to go in fairness?' a spokesperson rightly pointed out.

With almost two million separate greenways already completed this year, it is estimated greenways will outnumber the number of new homes five to one by next year.

#### Did You Know?
The High Kings of Ireland got their name from going at the mushrooms awful hard during the summer solstice.

Waterford Whispers News

## THE MIDDLE EAST

# LOCAL MAN ASKS PAKISTANI TAXI DRIVER TO EXPLAIN HISTORY OF MIDDLE EAST TENSIONS DURING 5-MINUTE TRIP INTO TOWN

AN EXTREMELY intoxicated Dublin man who hitherto had shown no interest in learning any details of various historical Middle Eastern and South Asian conflicts, has tasked his taxi driver for the evening with explaining it all in the time it takes to get from Phibsborough to Capel Street.

'Afghanistan? I'd say it was mental, not right Biden pulling out of your gaff,' offered Sean Glannon, in response to Pakistani taxi driver Sami Awan saying he was born in Islamabad.

'I'm looking for like the two-minute TikTok explainer, what's going down at all at all and why? The Gaza stuff, shoot, sound off, enlighten me,' urged Glannon, whose consumption of six cans plus no dinner combined to form the basis for a singular and fleeting interest in Middle East conflicts.

'That's mad, that's mad,' Glannon responded multiple times while his head was buried in his phone, prompting Awan to include several instances of completely made-up conflicts and flashpoints such as the 'Kebab Civil War' in his polite explanations.

Astonished and a little impressed by his own interest and wonderment, Glannon conceded privately that the Irish schooling system was to blame for not teaching him something that has been easily accessible on Wikipedia and other sources for over a decade.

'Who is it your lads don't like? Ha, no way, I thought you lads were basically the same? Ah the Brits split you in two, fucking preaching to the converted here man, say no more. Here, listen, I hope that all gets sorted anyway, sound,' Glannon said as he departed the taxi, before leaving Awan a three-star Free Now rating on account of talking too much.

> 'I'm looking for like the two-minute TikTok explainer, what's going down at all at all and why?'

### Community Alert

Heard from friend of a friend of one of the mams from school that white van with 500 immigrants is kidnapping 80 children a day – keep an eye out.

Local News

### HOUSING

# COUNCIL UNSURE IF DILAPIDATED BUILDING UNOCCUPIED FOR DECADE COUNTS AS 'VACANT' BUILDING

TASKED with identifying vacant properties within its boundaries, one local council is struggling significantly with the task despite the best will in the world.

'It's leaning to the left and looks like it could collapse if someone doesn't intervene soon,' a puzzled council worker shared with a colleague.

The building has been brought to the attention of the council on at least 10 occasions owing to the fact it was last occupied when the punt was still the official currency of Ireland.

'Yes, but on the other hand, judging by the rotting fox carcass we can see through the broken windows, it is likely occupied,' added the colleague. 'It's a shame that, would have been nice to find at least one building in this damned town that we could subject to the vacant sites levy.'

Deciding that the tree growing through the core of the building was intentionally put there by a visionary architect, the pair remained unable to spot any other potentially derelict buildings.

'The seven other buildings on this row seem to have the same interior decorator, what would you called that – "abandoned chic"? It's cool, not for my own place now but I like when owners make bold statements like that. No natural light due to boarding up the window, very "Berlin", isn't it?' offered the admiring council worker.

Noting that it was getting late, they agreed that they should probably head back to the office and start looking at vacant buildings again sometime in mid-2026.

> 'The seven other buildings on this row seem to have the same interior decorator'

### Classifieds

**LOST**

My son lost his medication in SuperValu car park late last night and it is very important to his wellbeing as he is suffering from a dose of that mental health thing that's been going around lately. They're speckled yellow in colour with a pharaoh stamp on them and may also be accompanied by his nasal powder and loose herbal tea.

Please contact Skinner's mother on 089-58796325 and ask for Skinner.

Waterford Whispers News

**BREAKING**

# 'KEEP GOING, IRELAND IS WITH YOU' COMMENTS DERANGED AUNT UNDER ENOCH BURKE ARTICLE

DERANGED LOCAL aunt Moira Kilcuddy has once again commented under a Facebook article reporting on Enoch Burke's ongoing incarceration, insisting, 'keep going, Ireland is with you'.

The comment marks the 437th consecutive article featuring the serial school gates loiterer that Kilcuddy has commented on, causing great embarrassment for her nieces and nephews.

'She commented "stay strong" under an article saying OJ Simpson has died. Name a person who is unworthy of support and you'll find Moira commenting up a blindly supportive storm, comparing them to Christ on the cross even if the local paper says they were caught trying to ride a squirrel,' said mortified niece Helen Kilcuddy.

'Everyone is praying for you', 'vote Enoch and Conor McGregor for Taoiseach and President' and 'a fine young man, I wish my lesbian haircutted niece would settle down with someone like you' were some of the least unhinged comments Kilcuddy insisted on leaving below articles on Facebook.

With her comments receiving a dearth of likes or positive emojis proving no barrier to the unyielding regularity of her comments, Kilcuddy seems to have an affinity for anyone who comes before the courts and proclaims themselves a victim of a corrupt legal system.

'Brilliant, having a good honest Irish man on that jury will make sure you're found not guilty, Donald,' added the 61-year-old aunt below a Fox News article on the hush money trial of Donald Trump, seemingly written as if the former US president himself would see her comment.

'I wouldn't mind her painful behaviour on social media so much, but she refused to write me a character reference when I was up in court for being wrongly accused of robbing the Spar, I wasn't even in the country at the time,' shared Kilcuddy's nephew, Sean Green.

**County Council Notices**

Yes the parking fees are atrocious and put off anyone from shopping in the city but at least they won't see the absolute state of the place.

Local News

## HEALTH

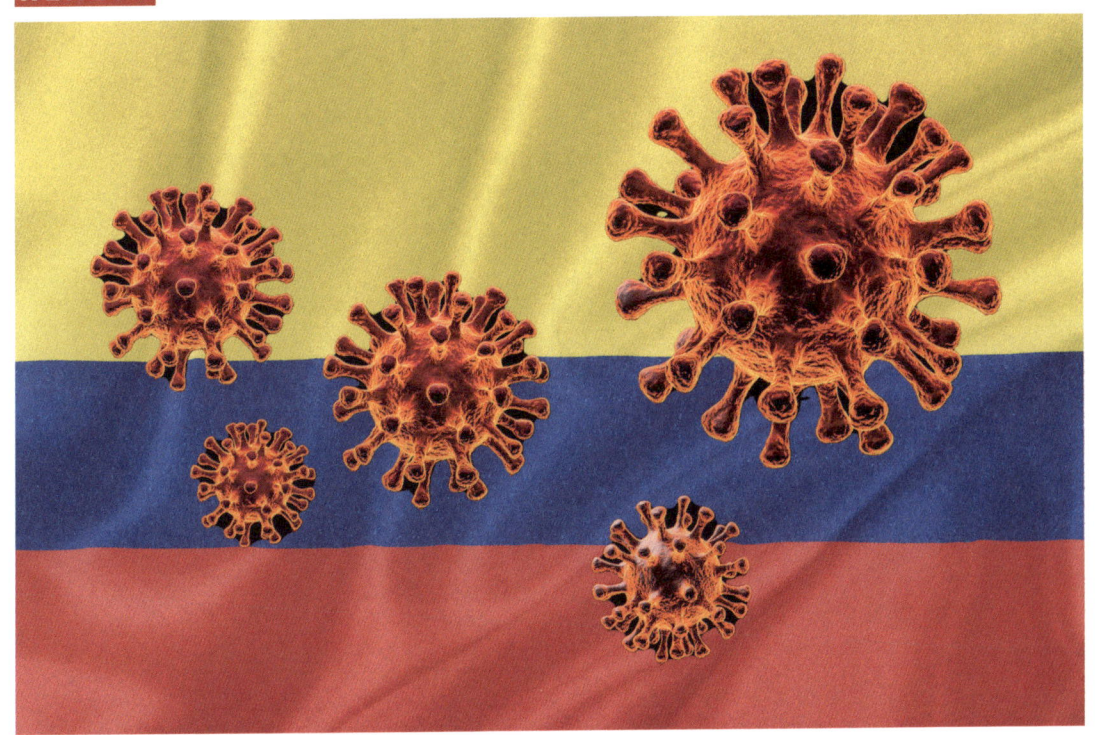

# HIGH INCIDENCE RATE OF THE COLOMBIAN FLU REPORTED ACROSS IRELAND

THE HSE has confirmed one of the highest incidence rates of any known virus is surging across the country. It's called the Colombian flu and is infecting all ages young and old, *WWN* reports.

Symptoms such as a runny nose, insomnia, extreme paranoia and loss of earnings have been reported in most cases, with a large number of people even fatally succumbing to the extreme strain.

'Symptoms usually start after a sip of alcohol, leading to a phone call and an immediate urge to run to the toilet,' Doctor Trevor Tracey describes the tell-tale signs. 'This is then followed by a numb feeling at the back of the throat, nonsensical conversations about mundane things and a propensity for extreme consumption of alcohol, leading to severe dehydration and dread over the next few days.'

> '**Symptoms usually start after a sip of alcohol, leading to a phone call and an immediate urge to run to the toilet**'

Doctors advised people to socially distance themselves from sufferers, as encountering them can result in the contagion spreading even more among groups of socialising friends.

'Especially avoid going to the toilet with people who have it as this seems to be where most people contract the Colombian flu,' a statement from the HSE warned.

Meanwhile, local pharmacist Decco Power claims that what makes you sick makes you better, and that he has been developing just the vaccine for the new variant.

'Just a little bump of this new vaccine before you head back into work on Monday morning will take the edge right off it,' he said. 'You can find my contact details on the back of any toilet door.'

### Did You Know?

A chicken once lived without its head for 18 months, a world record that has only ever been surpassed by the current sitting Irish government.

Waterford Whispers News

## PARENTING

# MOM SPARKS DEBATE AFTER SAYING SHE DOESN'T FEED HER KIDS LOCKED UP UNDER THE STAIRS

THIS mom refuses to feed her kids, who she keeps locked up under the stairs, and while she has her reasons for doing so, people have other opinions about this parenting method.

Jenna Hayes recently took to Instagram to talk about how people online keep questioning her parenting skills after posting a video of her children screaming for help behind a locked door situated under the stairs at her home.

'I understand she may have her reasons but as far as I know children need food to eat and this is probably wrong,' one person commented.

'I do this all the time with my lot. At least they've a roof over their heads. Well done, Jenna,' wrote another.

'LOL, I can hear them scratching at the door. That must get really annoying. I don't blame her at all, but yeah, she should probably feed them something,' added one Instagram user.

The post has gained thousands of comments on the app, with debate brewing over whether parents should be responsible for feeding children under the stairs.

'Kids these days want everything handed to them and I think locking them into a small space and starving them to death will make them better adults in later life,' one man said.

'Maybe show them some videos of starving children in Palestine and they might change their tune. Obviously spoilt little brats thinking they can have anything they want,' said another.

Should children locked under the stairs be given food and water? We'd love to hear your comments.

> 'As far as I know children need food to eat and this is probably wrong'

### Community Alert

Can we all keep the small talk in the estate down to brief mention of weather. No one gives a shit about your job or kids.

54

# ww news

Waterford Whispers News

# WORLD NEWS

Waterford Whispers News

## CLIMATE CHANGE

# EUROPE WARMING TWICE THE RATE OF OTHER CONTINENTS AND YOU'VE ALREADY STOPPED READING THIS HAVEN'T YOU

LEADING climate monitors have said Europe is warming at twice the rate of other continents and pointed to the 30% rise in heat-related deaths in the last 20 years as reason to immediately act and you checked out of this article long ago, didn't you?

'Have you considered being an ex-boyfriend of Taylor Swift's? Attending Victoria Beckham's 50th? Being the social media admin in charge of Nottingham Forest's X account?' These were some of the questions climate scientists were asked by PR specialists in a bid to help scientists get people's attention when issuing stark facts and projections, which will see climate refugees and extreme weather events dominate the twenty-first century and catastrophically upend societal cohesion.

'Is anyone listening? Thirty thousand people dying every year from heat-related deaths in Europe, 1.5 million people affected by floods in Slovenia last year,' a scientist said, trailing off because they knew full well you had moved on to a humorous video of a man in a gym accidentally dropping a kettle bell on his nads.

The body that produced the report, the Copernicus Climate Change Service, has been encouraged to consider a variety of tactics to gain the public's attention, including speaking in recycled Andrew Tate quotes, holding season five of *Stranger Things* ransom, entering the next *Love Island*, or starring in a viral video in which an adorably brave pig saves a baby goat from drowning in a pond.

Elsewhere, the Nobel Prize Committee has awarded climate scientists a prize for their pioneering and science-defying ability to appear invisible to the general public and politicians alike.

> 'Thirty thousand people dying every year from heat-related deaths in Europe'

**Famous Quotes from 2024**

"Mad! Same thing happened my friend Yevgeny"
– Putin upon hearing the death of Iranian President Ebrahim Raisi who was killed in a totally normal helicopter crash

World News

## UK ROYALTY

# DAILY MAIL STRUGGLING TO LINK MEGHAN MARKLE TO KING CHARLES'S CANCER

'I'M NOT sure anyone will believe the voodoo angle, Jane, but it's great you guys are thinking outside the box,' *Daily Mail* editor Jeremy Waynes told his team at a crisis meeting held this afternoon in Daily Mail HQ.

The 'all-hands-on-deck' meeting was called after Britain's most revered tabloid struggled to find a link between King Charles's recent cancer diagnosis and public enemy number one, Meghan Markle.

'The stress angle is too broad, guys, we need to pinpoint this right on her smug little American head,' Waynes elaborated once again, getting annoyed now that there isn't really much to connect the two, as though Markle was winning this one. 'Okay people, all I know is she's out there laughing at us now and hoping that Harry will take the throne somehow.'

With a five-hour brainstorming session failing to result in a concrete link, the team sieved through their ideas and barely contained racism one last time, hoping something would spark someone to come up with the most read story of the day.

'Nostradamus predicting his quick reign where Harry then becomes king, Camilla going in too hard with the butt plugs,

> 'Okay people, all I know is she's out there laughing at us now'

### Community Alert

Doing my bit to help housing crisis. Renting spare room – very hands off. Very reasonable €150 a week. Can't use kitchen, heat, front door or look me in the eye. Room available Sunday to Wednesday between hours of 6 a.m. and 2 p.m.

cancer may have been just down to genetics, a rich diet and old age? Okay, what lunatic thought of that last one? … John, you're now demoted to the Vulnerable Celebrities Looking Terrible department,' Waynes said, finally giving up but not before cursing Meghan Markle for getting away with the possible death of yet another monarch.

Waterford Whispers News

## RUSSIA

# US WARNS RUSSIAN ELECTION INTERFERENCE COULD SEE BOYD BARRETT NAMED FIRST TSAR OF IRELAND

OFFICIALS from the US State Department have spoken directly to the Irish Government in diplomatic cables to warn them that Russia's continued attempts to interfere in European democracies could affect Ireland and that authorities here should remain vigilant.

'We don't know who this Rickie Boy Barry guy is, but the Russians want him as their tsar in Ireland, we're talking a Soviet sickle on the tricolour folks, this is not a drill,' the diplomatic cable read.

'He is worshipped like some sort of god in some Russian cities; they have statues to him. If you don't stay on top of this stuff your richest 1% could be taxed at 178% on every euro they earn, he is already ruler of the notorious Communist commune known as Dún Laoghaire,' continued US officials.

Further warnings were issued about how Russian bot farms and online agitators could be used to further divide Irish society.

'These sorts of people try to say stuff like 200,000 people in Ireland are living in extremely deprived areas or talk about how despite a budget of €21bn the health service isn't fit for purpose, and how young people are locked out of home ownership and a decent standard of living,' warned a US official, highlighting how dangerous Russian trolls would evilly use up-to-date and accurate facts about Ireland.

While appreciative of the warning, the coalition Government confirmed, 'thanks but we don't need any additional help sowing further division in Irish society.'

### 2025 Predictions
Hundreds die in Mountjoy prison after the newly formed Cult of Enoch commits mass suicide after refusing to call a prison officer by their preferred pronoun.

# 'CAN'T GET A DECENT 3-IN-1 FOR LOVE NOR MONEY' TÁNAISTE CRITICISES CHINA DURING OFFICIAL VISIT

IRISH people may have feared Tánaiste Micheál Martin's trip to China would be void of tough talk on the big issues but it's clear from his latest comments that fear was unjustified and the Fianna Fáil man is perhaps owed an apology.

'Honestly, buck up your ideas, lads, it's a Chinese delicacy is it not? Cork is wiping the floor with ye,' Martin told Chinese Foreign Minister Wang Yi, in a clear and forceful rebuke of the nation's 3-in-1 standards.

'Fried rice, curry, chips; it's not rocket science, but when I asked for it down the Haidian District there last night everyone looked at me like I was looking for bat soup in a wet market,' added Martin to Chinese Vice President Han Zheng.

> 'Honestly, buck up your ideas lads, it's a Chinese delicacy is it not? Cork is wiping the floor with ye'

While the Irish public presumed Martin would eventually move on to bringing up the plight of Uyghur Muslims or the attempts to silence UCD academics whenever they speak on matters of Chinese history and current policies, Martin's ire remained fixed on the 'piss poor' quality of takeaway staples.

'We want our Irish beef exports to China to start up again, but honestly what's the point if your eateries are only going to butcher their attempts at a 3-in-1,' said Martin, his criticism laid bare and leaving Chinese officials in no doubt that Ireland will not stand for injustices of any kind.

## World News

### CLIMATE CHANGE

# 'CLIMATE BREAKDOWN HAS BEGUN' CLAIMS DRAMA QUEEN ANTÓNIO GUTERRES

UN SECRETARY-General and all-round drama queen António Guterres stated, 'our planet has just endured a season of simmering – the hottest summer on record. Climate breakdown has begun' in a wee bit of an overreaction.

Citing the release of data by the World Meteorological Organisation, which revealed Earth has experienced the hottest three-month period on record, Guterres was told to 'calm down' while others insisted it was just a case of 'his nerves being at him, he's always like this'.

'Ah, relax, we always get pure lovely Septembers,' reassured one Irish person, when it was pointed out that the US has suffered just shy of 20 individual billion-dollar disasters so far this year, including wildfires, floods, heatwaves and storms.

'Who's a panicking Polly, sure wasn't it lashing here all July, couldn't move for rain but the planet's never been hotter? Does UN stand for Unusually Nervous?' offered another local who will be evacuated from their summer holidays next year due to wildfires.

Guterres is once again pleading with world leaders to act now and increase emission-curbing targets so that future climate disasters can be averted.

'Someone's got his knickers in a twist,' confirmed another person, having already forgotten that the earthquake in Turkey and Syria affected 15 million people, destroyed over 300,000 apartments and killed 50,000 people.

Elsewhere, one wise local told Guterres the key to achieving a huge reduction in carbon emissions overnight is 'racism'. 'Just tell everyone if we don't avert climate breakdown now, climate disaster refugees will end up in your local town, simple,' confirmed the man.

---

### County Council Notices

Thanks to an increase in the arts budget we're proud to announce we have enough funding to pay 10 arts students filled with regret over their life choices to dance about a bit on the quays this weekend.

---

### Mindlessness Tip

Think POSITIVE: Properly Overthinking Shit, Internally Terrified, Indulging Volatile Emotions

Waterford Whispers News

## RELIGION

# GOD AND SATAN FINALLY RECONCILE DIFFERENCES FOLLOWING HISTORIC PEACE TALKS IN GENEVA

FOLLOWING aeons of conflict causing countless deaths, wars and civil unrest, God the Almighty has announced he is to allow fallen angel Lucifer back into heaven after eventually reconciling their differences during historic peace talks held in Geneva this week.

The pair rekindled their friendship at the three-day summit, agreeing to scrap hell altogether and 'start over' with a 'clean slate'.

'We just took things up where we left off really, it's like we never fell out,' the now reinstated angel Lucifer stated, who confirmed he is to move back home later this week once he obliterates the fiery pits of hell.

However, the news has received mixed reactions from religious entities on Earth, with the Vatican stating it is now left in limbo, with its entire revenue stream put in jeopardy.

'No more confessions, communions, redemption of sins, what are we supposed to do now if there's no good or evil? How will we control our worshippers, or milk them for money?' a senior cardinal told *WWN*.

'The old man has gone soft,' echoed the archangel Gabriel, who has sat on the right-hand side of the Lord 'since day one'. 'That prick Lucifer better not put one foot wrong or I'll clip his wings very fast, let me tell you – I'll be watching him like a hawk.'

> '**No more confessions, communions, redemption of sins, what are we supposed to do now if there's no good or evil?'**

It is expected that any souls currently residing in hell will be vaporised into nothingness immediately, with the future of those still on Earth yet to be decided.

'The big man said he wants to go back to basics and mentioned something about reintroducing dinosaurs to the Earth for the craic to see what happens,' a heavenly spokesperson confirmed.

**Community Alert**

Everyone needs to sign the petition Graham Harney sent round NOW! They're trying to build houses around the corner. Can you believe the fucking cheek?

60

# World News

## THE MIDDLE EAST

# VON DER LEYEN SHOWS FULL SUPPORT FOR ISRAEL BY LEADING GAZA BOMBING MISSION

HEAD OF THE European Commission Ursula von der Leyen is facing further claims that she is overstepping the remit of her office in her expressions of unequivocal EU support for Israel and its actions, this time manning a fighter jet that is raining down bombs on Gaza.

Leading with a no-nonsense thumbs up and a calm but firm 'Israel has the right to defend itself', von der Leyen climbed into the cockpit of an Israeli F-16 fighter jet in a move that could yet again frustrate EU leaders and officials who have reminded the German politician that she does not speak for the EU on foreign policy matters.

'She can offer Israel the EU's unconditional support for any breach of international law in much the same way a banana can teach a hippo to fly,' actual EU foreign policy

> 'She can offer Israel the EU's unconditional support for any breach of international law in much the same way a banana can teach a hippo to fly'

chief Josep Borrell stated. 'EU foreign policy is an inter-governmental decision, she's overstepped the mark like … hmmm, can I think of a good example? Eh, oh like a country cutting off power, water and fuel while bombing civilian targets.' Seemingly unable to break her current streak of speaking on behalf of others in matters she has no authority over, von der Leyen has said that Taylor Swift

### Mindlessness Tip

It was a fox. You hit a fox. Just keep telling yourself it was a fox. It's definitely fox fur caught in the grille and not human ginger hair. Maybe get the bus for the next while just to be safe.

must end her relationship with NFL player Travis Kelce. She has named Idris Elba as the next James Bond and confirmed that Longford native Eileen Neary's kitchen is getting an overdue remodelling whether she likes it or not.

'Oops, was that a hospital?' confirmed von der Leyen as she raced through the skies over Gaza.

**Waterford Whispers News**

## RUSSIA

# 'TECHNICALLY DRAGO BEAT ROCKY TO A PULP': ALL THE HOT TAKES FROM THE PUTIN INTERVIEW

IN WHAT is being hailed by your weird-smelling uncle as the Russian President's toughest interview to date, WWN has compiled all the hot takes from Tucker Carlson's grilling of the most elusive world leader of the twenty-first century, Vladimir Vladimirovich Putin.

'I thought Joe Rogan had no hair and looked like a boiled ham pumped full of steroids?' This was Putin's reaction to first meeting Tucker Carlson.

'Definitely in the fridge,' Putin replied when Tucker asked a no-holds-barred question about where he keeps the ketchup. A clear indication this would not be an interview full of softball questions.

'There is no doubt in my mind that Apple continues to slow down older phones to force your hand to buy a new one,' Putin claimed as he demonstrated to Carlson with two iPhones charging together. 'This is criminal, yet the West continues to turn a blind eye.'

'This interview is gu-lagging a bit. Maybe I should talk about sixteenth-century Russian history again?' Putin suggested, when asked about the Nord Stream pipeline.

'I suppose they'll be calling you Cucker Tarlson now?' Putin jested, forcing Carlson to giggle like a schoolgirl with a crush.

In a heated exchange, Putin slammed Carlson's suggestion that Rocky beat Drago in the movie *Rocky IV*, stating the Russian boxer was far superior in strength, speed and boxing abilities. A two-hour break had to be called by the production team to allow both men to calm down.

'I know you are, but what am I?' Putin cleverly deflected when asked if he thought fixing elections and changing laws to keep in him power indefinitely was 'a little bit dictatory'.

> **'I'm listening to some old-school Czech industrial techno in my earpiece – it keeps me calm'**

'I'm listening to some old-school Czech industrial techno in my earpiece – it keeps me calm,' said Putin, revealing why his feet were tapping right through the entire two-hour interview.

'*The Wire* – all day. *Sopranos* second, then *Breaking Bad*,' he replied to a question about his top TV series of all time, before then going on about how the story of Tony Soprano's crew paralleled the Kingdom of Poland and the Grand Duchy of Lithuania of the 1600s.

World News

## UK ROYALTY

# 'I USED THE BLOOD SPILLED BY BRITISH EMPIRE TO GET THE REDS' CHARLES PORTRAITIST EXPLAINED

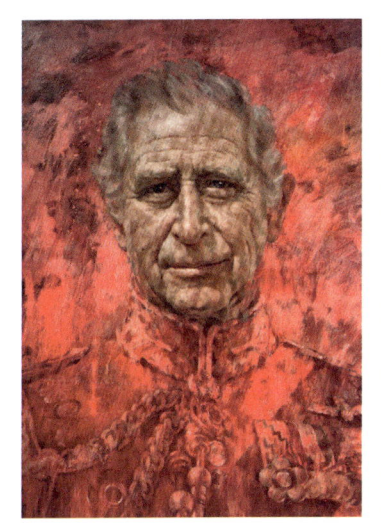

UNVEILING a portrait of Britain's King Charles that is set to fuel the nightmares of millions of people around the world, the artist behind the poor imitation of the painting in *Ghostbusters II* has spoken on the labour-intensive process that brought the portrait to life.

'I thought it was a nice nod to the royal family and British history,' said painter Jonathan Yeo, who conjured up the evocative and distinctive reds in the portrait by using the vats of blood from those slain in the name of the royal family, which are stored in the basements of several royal palaces.

Sources close to the palace said it was a rare honour for Yeo to be allowed to use the blood as it's normally reserved for ritualistic ceremonies or in attempts to reanimate the Queen.

The painting has provoked a strong reaction from the public, with some people who have viewed it saying they felt they could hear the screams of the dying, something which was intentional as a series of speakers set up in the room piped in the last known recording of various massacres and atrocities perpetrated by British forces.

'The deathly soulless demeanour of the King was all Charles, I can't take credit for that,' added Yeo, who in a meta quality ensured that all the brushes and canvas he used were stolen from former colonies.

# ICC CONFIRMS IT HAS FUNCTIONING EYESIGHT

PROSECUTORS at the International Criminal Court have been told that they can put off their eyesight test for at least another 12 months after they asked the ICC to issue a number of arrest warrants, including one for Benjamin Netanyahu who they contend has committed the crime of starvation of a people as well as extermination and murder of Palestinians.

'Yup, we have eyes,' confirmed prosecutors who have charged Israel's Minister for Defence Yoav Gallant alongside Netanyahu for orchestrating hell on earth in Gaza, while issuing separate charges for Hamas's Yahya Sinwar for his role in the 7 October massacre and subsequent kidnapping of hundreds of Israelis.

'We just used our eyes,' stressed prosecutors when pressed by mystified western media outlets as to what masterful levels of deduction and intelligence they used, which has prevented sections of the media from calling what is unfolding a genocide.

Were ICC judges to grant the arrest warrants, Netanyahu has complained the number of countries he can holiday in would be greatly hindered, which is the 'greatest crime of all'.

Elsewhere, opticians confirmed that US politicians have tested en masse for a rare congenital eye condition called 'selective blind eye turning'.

UPDATE: The ICC has belatedly apologised for booking in laser eye surgery on the same day George Bush's administration pretended Iraq had weapons of mass destruction as justification for launching an invasion.

### 2025 Predictions
More extreme weather events resulting in death and destruction will perplex people who hate hearing the words 'climate' and 'change'.

### Mindlessness Tip
Spread a rumour about a popular colleague in work and watch your happiness increase as their life slowly unravels.

Waterford Whispers News

### EXCLUSIVE

# GOING TO LIVE IN THE MARIANA TRENCH SO YOU NEVER HAVE TO HEAR THE WORD 'WOKE' AGAIN

A LEADING tour operator and mental health specialist have joined forces to offer customers the chance to avoid ever having to hear people ceaselessly bleat on and on about 'wokeism'.

A term derisively employed by everyone from Joe Rogan to the *Daily Mail* to the uncle your family no longer has any dealings with to floundering politicians in power who need a scapegoat to distract from their failings, 'woke' is the word that people just can't escape. That is, until now.

'We usually specialise in cruises where you can pop to the Caribbean for a spot of snorkelling, but we're taking it one step further for those customers who think they'll go insane if they have to hear another person claim children are identifying as cats in school,' shared tour operator Could Murder A Holiday, showing off a new submersible which will leave people rooted 2km below the ocean's surface.

'Research shows us that this is the only place you'll be safe from a divorced dad's X rant about gay marriage or your ex asking, "when's International Men's Day, though?" and we think €50,000 is a reasonable fee to pay for escaping the dreaded W word,' explained joint head of the project, psychologist Dr Murna Doyle.

The vessel contains enough food to last 20 years, which is the estimated time the *Daily Mail* will finally tire of using the word, meaning a person's dream of escaping tiresome and clichéd moaning is within their grasp.

> 'Research shows us that this is the only place you'll be safe from a divorced dad's X rant about gay marriage'

UPDATE:
A spokesperson for Could Murder A Holiday has apologised to customers on the maiden voyage to the bottom of the Mariana Trench after a stowaway who is only capable of repeating the phrase 'cancel culture' sneaked on board.

### Classifieds

**VACANCIES – RECEPTIONIST WANTED**

Soulless middle-aged woman wanted as receptionist at a local doctor's surgery. Must have a resting bitch face. Zero people skills essential. Wears musty perfume and owns a cardigan from the 1970s.
Call Ballyfail Medical Centre on 051-568547895

World News

## THE MIDDLE EAST

# IDF CLEARS ITSELF OF WRONGDOING FOR 27,677TH DAY IN A ROW

FOLLOWING a thorough examination of all available evidence, there was widespread relief as IDF spokesperson Daniel Hagari confirmed the IDF has fully cleared the IDF of all involvement in the deaths of starving Palestinians seeking food from an aid convoy.

'That's a relief, we don't have to even bother investigating. Despite the IDF's many conflicting statements on the incident, in which they initially said they didn't fire on people, then confirmed they did, I'm convinced,' confirmed the US government, alongside other key allies.

This fact-finding mission on the possible wrongdoing of Israeli forces marks the 27,677th successive day the IDF has cleared the IDF of any responsibility or error since its foundation in 1948.

'I suppose we're lucky to have an organisation such as the IDF checking this stuff out or else we'd never know the IDF is innocent of all crimes the IDF is accused of. You start to wonder whether we even need guys like the International Criminal Court,' said one netizen, who can sleep soundly tonight knowing the IDF has never put a foot wrong.

This latest ironclad and unbiased verdict joins a long and illustrious list of IDF innocence including the murder of journalist Shireen Abu Akleh, the bulldozing of American activist Rachel Corrie, the 2014 bombings in Gaza resulting in the murder of four boys as they played football on the beach and the attack on US naval ship the USS *Liberty*, which killed 34 people, among thousands of other incidents of complete innocence.

UPDATE: The IDF has today claimed it has gathered further proof of the involvement of UNRWA staff in the 7 October massacre, news which has come at an inconvenient time as it risks moving the media's attention away from the deaths of over 100 Palestinians killed as they converged on an aid convoy.

'This is just awful timing, our initial claims of UNRWA involvement came a day after the IDF was accused of bombing a UN refugee camp and killing 20 civilians,' confirmed IDF spokesperson Daniel Hagari.

### County Council Notices

We understand the frustration over several preachers preaching in the city centre but to be honest if you people were a little more God-like they wouldn't have to do this.

### The Year in Numbers

**13** The number of former BT Young Scientist award winners who now work in the underground lair of an evil billionaire hellbent on world domination.

65

Waterford Whispers News

## THE MIDDLE EAST

# US TELLS ISRAEL IT WON'T JOIN STRIKES ON IRAN, JUST PROFIT FROM THEM

'GOD NO, Benny, we're just here to incite tensions and make trillions of dollars from the proceeds,' US Foreign Secretary Antony J. Blinken told Israeli Prime Minister Benjamin Netanyahu last night in a brief phone call, which followed a series of Iranian airstrikes on the world's most unfortunate nation.

'Strategically we need you guys right there in the thick of it, hence why we've given you guys a quarter trillion since '47, a nice glitzy iron dome and allowed you to genocide the beejesus out of Palestinians for the past 70-odd years, but as far as us going to war against those mad fuckers in Iran – not a hope,' he added, before asking how many more fighter jets Israel wanted this month.

Iran fired over 300 drones and missiles at Israel on Sunday, stating it was in response to a 1 April strike on its consulate in Syria; however, just 1% of its bombs made it through, which according to experts made Iran look 'a bit outdated when it comes to this war craic'.

'If it comes to it we'll throw in a few F-35s free of charge this month and a few thousand of those 50-cal sniper rifles your guys love shooting Palestinian kids with,' Blinken told the Israeli PM, before quickly winding up the call. 'Sorry, I've the Z man calling me on the other line from Kyiv here looking to make an order, Ben, give us a shout next week … yeah, it's all go these days, no rest for the wicked as they say but sure we're making a killing. Chat soon.'

> 'If it comes to it we'll throw in a few F-35s free of charge this month and a few thousand of those 50 cal sniper rifles your guys love shooting Palestinian kids with'

**Did You Know?**
It's a war crime if Russia is the one doing it, but not a war crime if Israel is the one doing it.

**Community Alert**
Ardcrillen Residents' Association stands by its decision to place land mines at the most popular dog fouling spots in the locality.

## SCOTLAND
# 1.2 MILLION ARRESTED IN SCOTLAND ON FIRST DAY OF NEW HATE SPEECH LAW

OVER one-fifth of the population of Scotland was arrested on the first day of the new hate speech law yesterday, sparking fears that there will be no one left on the outside if the trend continues.

Courts up and down the country were packed to the rafters with people convicted of hate speech as the controversial new law took effect yesterday morning, crippling the nation and bringing it to a halt.

'If this keeps up the economy could collapse within days,' government sources told WWN.

Senior police officers said they can't keep up with complaints regarding online posts, with a huge backlog expected to see most of the Scottish nation accused of hate speech and locked up in a cell by the weekend.

The Hate Crime and Public Order (Scotland) Act 2021 creates a new crime of 'stirring up hatred' relating to age, disability, religion, sexual orientation and transgender identity, with a maximum penalty of seven years.

'I was only slaggin',' one Glaswegian man accused of hate speech told a judge today. 'I slag everyone off, how can I be accused of hating just one group of people when I actually hate them all equally?'

Meanwhile closer to home, Justice Minister Helen McEntee reassured the public that the Irish version of the law will only affect people the Government doesn't agree with.

# EU TO PLACE SANCTIONS ON IRAN FOR BOMBING COUNTRY THAT KILLED 30,000 CIVILIANS

SHOWING that no attack goes without serious financial punishment unless Palestinians are the target or victims, EU leaders pledged to impose further sanctions on Iran in the wake of a series of drone attacks aimed at Israel.

'Let this be proof that the EU will act swiftly and decisively to call out and punish unjustified and illegal aggression with sanctions when it's aimed at non-Gazan locations,' confirmed Josep Borrell, the EU's foreign affairs chief.

'What right-minded and moral person would be okay with attempts to rain fire down on innocent women and children? Well, in the case of Gaza, us, but aside from that we're happy to hit the sanctions button. How can we maintain a rules-based order in the world and have peace flourish if nations think they can just bomb a location without any consequences?' added Borrell, not talking about Israel razing Gaza to the ground, killing over 30,000 people and counting in the process.

EU leaders were careful not to be drawn on turning the loss of human life into a tawdry exercise in maths due in part because 'our maths doesn't add up if you place the same value on Palestinian lives as every other human being.'

'We cannot have unprecedented attacks like this,' added EU leaders, the vast majority of whom are perfectly happy to see the planned and targeted murdering of innocent civilians go unpunished if it's Benjamin Netanyahu doing it.

Waterford Whispers News

## THE MIDDLE EAST

# US CALLS FOR GAZA CEASEFIRE TO ALLOW TIME TO MANUFACTURE MORE WEAPONS TO SELL ISRAEL

DESPERATELY trying to keep up with Israel's demand for weapons to annihilate the Palestinian people, the US has graciously asked for a ceasefire for a few weeks to allow time for the manufacturing process.

US Vice President Kamala Harris has demanded that Hamas agree to an immediate six-week ceasefire, if any of them are left, and politely urged Israel to act like it's giving aid to Gaza without murdering people in cold blood before rolling over them in tanks again.

'Seriously, our arms factories are stretched with the demand from all the world conflicts we've started and our contractors are struggling to produce all these freedom makers to give them a chance to catch up,' Harris explained, apologising to customers on behalf of Lockheed Martin and Boeing, whose profits have soared in recent years thanks to US foreign policy. 'We'd like to profusely apologise to Mr Netanyahu and all of our customers abroad for the delay, but producing weapons of mass destruction takes time; why not use some white phosphorus in the interim? We won't mind.'

With fears that hundreds of thousands of Palestinians may still survive Israel's ongoing genocide, the starvation of the remaining Palestinian survivors is now the Zionists' best hope of resurrecting those killed in October and securing the safe return of any remaining Israeli hostages.

'Killing 40,000, mostly innocent women and children, is guaranteed to never come back to bite us on the arse,' an IDF source said in explaining his reasoning, before casually blowing off a child's head with his sniper rifle.

# RISK ELDERLY PRESIDENTIAL CANDIDATES WILL FORGET TO BRING UP OPPONENT'S POOR MEMORY

POLITICAL strategists in America fear their advice on the weaknesses of the two respective presidential front-runners will go unheeded, in large part due to the fact that the ailing advertisements for Alzheimer's research, Joe Biden and Donald Trump, will struggle to remember to bring up their opponent's poor memory.

In the wake of a Republican special council declining to bring charges against Biden for retaining classified documents from his time as vice-president, due to the fact he felt a jury would not convict Biden on account of being 'elderly and having a poor memory', the opportunity to chip away at his credibility is wide open for Trump, if he could concentrate for longer than 30 seconds.

'We set up that nakedly partisan hatchet job so we could use this in attack ads, we workshopped what phrase to use ('elderly with poor memory') but does Donald bring it up on stage? No, he starts weeping about Taylor Swift and the fucking NFL,' said one Republican strategist, now weeping himself.

'Trump has in recent months said his opponent in the upcoming 2024 election is Barack Obama and mistaken Nikki Haley for Nancy Pelosi. Do you think we can get Biden to remember to bring this up when he's on the campaign? Hah!' said one exhausted strategist for the Democrats.

According to these strategists, it is the great tragedy of the forthcoming election campaign that never have two candidates given their opponents so much to ridicule the other over but each been simultaneously so cognitively corroded to the point that they have to wear name badges to remind themselves of who they are.

'We spent months reminding Joe to bring up the fact Trump mistakenly identified E. Jean Carroll as his ex-wife in a photo during a deposition, but he's too busy mistakenly identifying Mexico as Egypt in press interviews,' said the latest strategist, leading him to to up and quit on the spot.

'Face it, these ageing asshats think the hippocampus is grazing in a shallow watering hole in the Serengeti.'

World News

## SANTA CLAUS INC

# 'WE'RE BANKRUPT' – REVENUE HITS SANTA WITH MASSIVE TOY IMPORT TAX BILL

**Famous Quotes from 2024**

"For all that is sacred in this world, please stop drinking them like it's a mega pint of Buckfast" - **Emmanuel Macron, on Irish Olympic team supporters in Paris and their wine-drinking habits**

FINNISH toy manufacturer and distributor Santa Claus Inc has gone into receivership today after being hit with a huge import tax bill, *WWN* has learned.

Spokesman and CEO Santa Claus has stated he was given just seven days to pay arrears of over two trillion dollars in VAT on goods he imported over a 300-year period.

'We're fucked,' Mr Claus briefed staff at his Lapland headquarters in Finland earlier. 'We're bankrupt, Revenue have taken our deer and will be back for the rest of our assets in the morning if we don't pony up.'

Trading as a global operation since the late 1700s, Santa Inc will now be handed over to a board of receivers in a bid to salvage the company and keep at least 20% of its workforce.

'Free toys will obviously be the first thing we scrap,' a source said. 'We're also going to move operations to Bangladesh to keep costs down.'

It is understood that Mr Claus will also face legal proceedings and could receive five to ten years in prison for tax evasion.

> 'We're bankrupt, Revenue have taken our deer and will be back for the rest of our assets in the morning'

**Mindlessness Tip**

Anxious about returning to work after the Christmas holidays? Start a rumour that your office is going to house refugees so 'concerned locals' will burn it down.

69

Waterford Whispers News

## THE MIDDLE EAST

# ISRAEL RECOGNISES BRITAIN'S RIGHT TO THE 26 COUNTIES

IN A dramatic retort to Ireland recognising the state of Palestine, Israel has gone one better and officially recognised Britain's right to the Irish Republic's 26 counties, opening old wounds between the states.

Ireland, Spain and Norway have announced today they will formally recognise a Palestinian state on 28 May, triggering the immediate response from Israel, which recalled its ambassadors from Dublin and Oslo before childishly claiming Ireland is British.

'Yeah, well we recognise you as belonging to Britain, so there!' stated Israeli Foreign Minister Israel Katz, unveiling a map of Ireland covered in a Union Jack. 'Cillian Murphy, Saoirse Ronan, that big bog-headed man from the Banshee thing; all fucking English, you pricks.' Israel has also called for a nationwide ban on the colour green, Guinness and anything that could be conceived as Irish from the Jewish state, with reports of homeowners now dying their grass blue in disgust at the Emerald Isle's decision to recognise another state being illegally occupied by an imperial force.

### County Council Notices

For those inquiring about the regional building inspector position, you are correct in your assumption there's no point in applying as someone in the office thinks that'll be a handy number for their husband.

### Classifieds

**INCARCERATE BRITNEY**

Now I know I was on here a few years ago banging on about freeing Britney Spears from her conservatorship, but it looks like we were seriously wrong about the whole thing what with her antics on social media. I've since apologised to her father James and vowed to undo everything by launching a campaign to have her put back under her father's control.

Meeting in the local hall at 8 p.m.

World News

**MIGRATION**

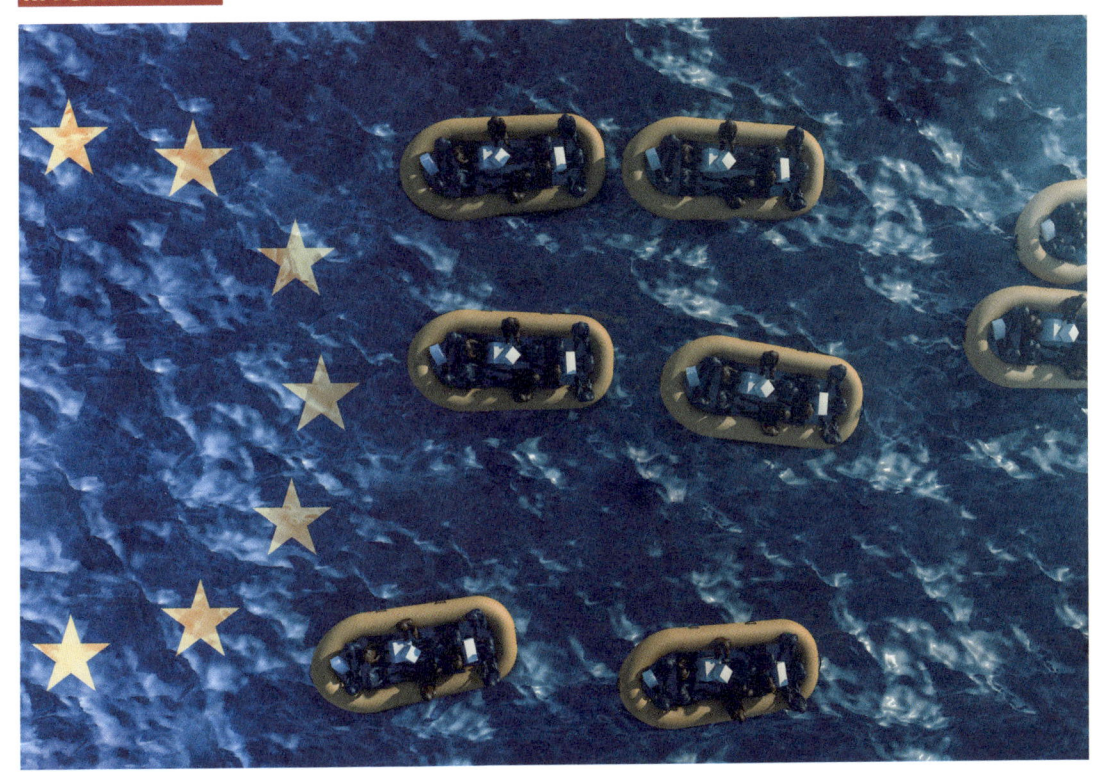

# PROS & CONS OF THE EU'S NEW ASYLUM AND MIGRATION PACT

IN CONTRAST to the protests and demonstrations in Brussels after MEPs voted through a new asylum seeker and migration pact, which was negotiated over the last eight years, others were celebrating EU Member States finally agreeing on how to deal with migration.

Weighing up the proposals, which include speeding up decisions on claims made by asylum seekers and ensuring all countries share responsibility for asylum applications:

**PRO:** MEPs got to claim some travel expenses for the vote.
**CON:** A large percentage of Europeans actually asked for a ceasefire in Gaza, but okay.

**PRO:** You can ignore the human suffering, which is a cornerstone of western prosperity, for a little longer.

**CON:** This will further erode the human rights of those seeking refuge, which aren't currently being enforced in the first place.

**PRO:** If you're sufficiently naive you'll blissfully believe this will reduce the number of refugees drowning in the Mediterranean, a number that stands at 30,000 over the last 10 years.
**CON:** You'll vomit in your mouth a little if you catch sight of Ursula von der Leyen saying this pact protects vulnerable people.

**PRO:** Instead of having your tax go to paying Irish hoteliers to house asylum seekers because the Government hasn't bothered to create purpose-built asylum centres, your tax money can now go to paying an African dictator or two to police the EU's borders and imprison and torture refugees.

**CON:** Your far-right uncle thinks this pact, which has been criticised by every refugee NGO across Europe for being inhumane and a backwards step, is in fact a secret plan enacted by NGOs to flood Gort with 40 million unvetted males.

**PRO:** Irish media outlets bored of running stories claiming 'it costs Ireland €3 trillion a second to house asylum seekers' can now change their claims to, 'Outrageous Government using taxpayers' money to pay EU so they don't have to take more asylum seekers.' And that lovely holiday to Greece you have planned stands less chance of leaving a bitter taste in the mouth.
**CON:** This won't stop Tommy Robinson crossing the Irish Sea to meet up with members of the Irish far right.

Waterford Whispers News

## US POLITICS

# TRUMP CAN'T FATHOM WHY BIDEN WOULD PUT COUNTRY BEFORE HIS OWN SELF-INTEREST

'I DON'T GET IT' said an upset and confused Donald Trump, as his inner circle tried to explain concepts including integrity, selflessness and the greater good: motivations and obligations that may have driven Joe Biden to announce that he will not be standing in the US presidential election.

In a rare lucid moment, Joe Biden announced that he would not be accepting the Democratic nomination for president, marking the first time he has formed a fully coherent sentence since his disastrous performance in his debate with Trump.

> 'So you're telling me he was running for president to serve the people, and improve things? What a loser'

'So you're telling me he was running for president to serve the people, and improve things? What a loser,' offered Trump, incredulous at the stupidity displayed by his political rival, who was walking away from the sort of golden opportunity the Republican would use to further enrich himself.

Biden had initially tried to stay the course after some left-leaning media outlets kindly described his debate performance as 'struggled at times and stumbled over his words' rather than the more accurate reporting of 'it was like watching a dog trying to do complex math while climbing a ladder made of cheese'.

'Why didn't he just appoint his son president or something?'

### County Council Notices

Last warning – you can't just walk around the town, enjoy the fresh air and grab a seat on a bench if you're not spending money. Local amenities like parks aren't meant for that carry on.

Trump added, his brain swelling due to the difficulty of comprehending someone not acting in naked self-interest.

Biden's decision has sparked potential Democratic nominees into action, with dozens and dozens of senior figures in the party letting all calls from one such person, Hillary Clinton, go straight to voicemail.

Elsewhere, not content with putting America before his own self-interest, Biden has confirmed that for the remainder of his presidency he will put Israeli war crimes before innocent Palestinian lives.

### 2025 Predictions

2025 is the year Satan retires and hands over the reins to Rupert Murdoch.

World News

### THE MIDDLE EAST

# ISRAELI ARMY RELEASES X-RAYS PROVING HAMAS HIDING INSIDE PALESTINIAN CHILDREN

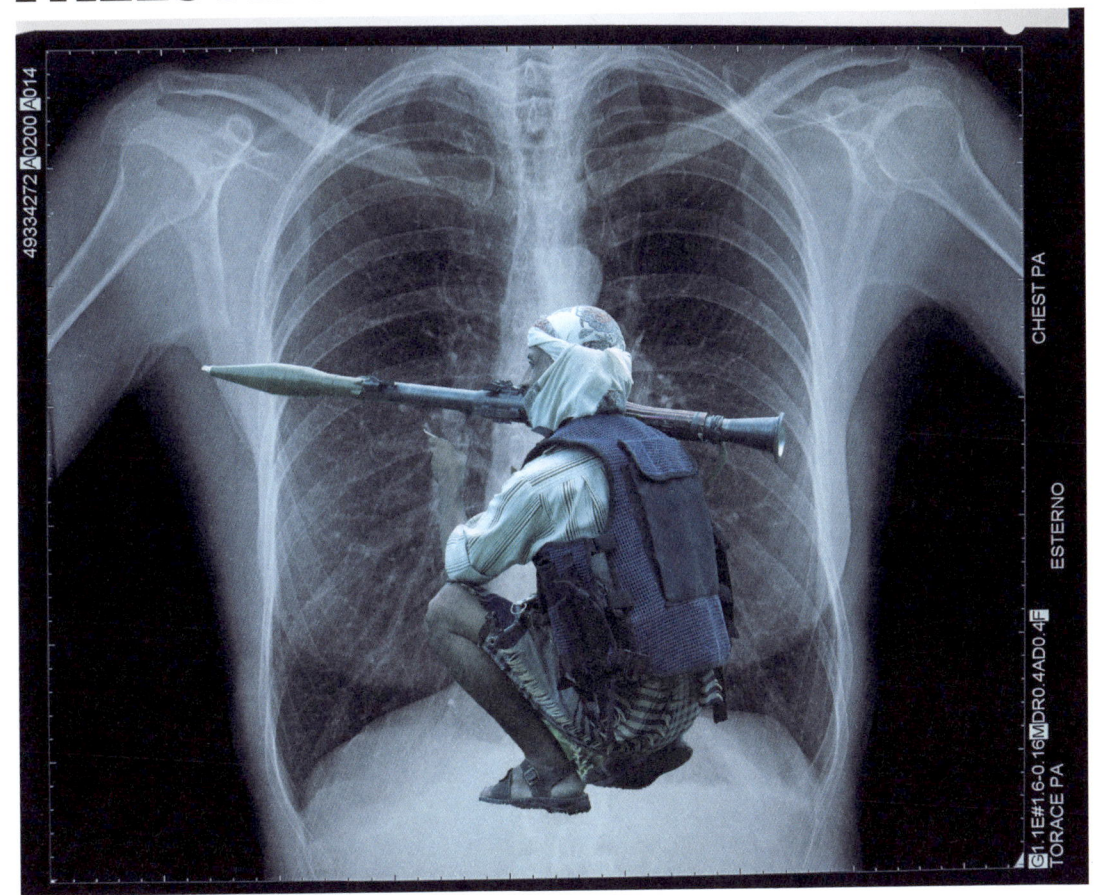

'SEE? We told you they were hiding inside children all this time but you wouldn't believe us, now here's the proof!' an IDF spokeskiller told the international media today after unveiling a series of X-rays found during a raid at a Palestinian hospital.

**Mindlessness Tip**
Playing out an ongoing argument with your partner in your head is a great way of distracting yourself from important work deadlines that you must have completed by today.

Publishing the pictures online for the world to see, a fully armoured Hamas terrorist brandishing an AK-47 can be seen hiding out in a small child's chest cavity, presumably waiting to pounce at any moment on unsuspecting Israelis dozens of kilometres away behind the safety of a sophisticated Iron Dome defence system.

'It's not just children either; entire Hamas cells have been hiding out in elderly men and women too, giving us no choice now but to obliterate them for harbouring terrorists,' the IDF added. 'We'll try to just kill the terrorists inside the children, but we can't make any promises about saving their lives.'

With the Gaza death toll currently nearing 40,000, the IDF estimates at least twice that number of Hamas terrorists have also been killed while hiding deep inside so-called innocent civilians.

'We believe that a lot of the Hamas terrorists may have also escaped the bodies of the children we've already killed and found new Palestinian hosts to hide in,' the IDF continued. 'We'll just have to keep targeting these little flesh shields until they're all gone.'

Waterford Whispers News

## RELIGION

# 'DON'T BLAME ME' – GOD DENIES SAVING TRUMP

GOD ALMIGHTY has broken millennia of silence to clarify events surrounding the assassination attempt on Donald Trump, feeling he now needs to speak out as fervent and deranged Republican-voting Christians claim that he personally spared Trump's life.

'You idiots ask for a sign, and when I give you one; a rally held in the open, lax security, a clear shot from a nearby roof, you still don't get it?' explained God in a hastily arranged press conference.

'And so I don't want other people blaming me for saving him, I tried my best.'

Hailing divine intervention and feting him at the Republican national convention, supporters and acolytes sought to deify their presidential nominee and anoint him as a living saint.

'Oh, you need three miracles to become canonised, right?' retorted God, 'so we've got one, slept with a porn star while his wife was pregnant; two, committing fraud with his businesses; and three, demonising and vilifying those in need, that's the trifecta there alright.'

The convention also saw Trump appoint JD Vance as his running mate for the elections.

'Well I'll at least credit him for forgiving Vance for calling him America's Hitler, "reprehensible" and a "moral disaster". Also, while I have your attention, America, my son does not have white skin and blue eyes,' said God, concluding the press conference.

### Did You Know?
Steven Seagal has never acted in a movie.

### The Year in Numbers
**400,000**
Tonnes of carbon emissions generated by Taylor Swift's private jet ferrying Leo Burdocks from Dublin to her New York home.

**World News**

**US POLITICS**

# UNCLEAR WHAT IT IS ABOUT MIXED-RACE WOMAN RUNNING FOR PRESIDENT THAT HAS TRUMP SUPPORTERS SO AGITATED

POLITICAL experts are scratching their heads trying to find the precise reasons former US president Donald Trump and his devotees have reacted so strongly to the news that Kamala Harris, a woman of Asian and Jamaican heritage, is the likely Democratic nominee for president in the wake of Joe Biden exiting the race.

'It's undemocratic to parachute her into his place after Democrats voted for Biden in the primaries,' shared one Trump Republican, showcasing a rare respect for votes cast in an election.

'She's uppity, shrill, aggressive, manly and unqualified' said a Republican senator consulting his *Racist Dog Whistles for Sexists Beginners' Handbook*.

Such comments have left large US media outlets to muse endlessly over the unknowable motivation behind some Trump Republicans' distaste for Harris.

'What about when she was district attorney in San Francisco and her office prosecuted innocent black man Jamal Trulove for a murder it was clear he did not commit?' said another Trump supporter who would normally see such things as a reason to vote for someone.

'If she becomes president, she'll flood the US border with brown people in a plan to destroy the pure white bloodline of true Christian Americans. It's time to bring back sundown towns,' added another Republican, in comments which were worded in such a vague and meandering way as to make identifying the ideology behind the sentiments impossible.

> 'If she becomes president, she'll flood the US border with brown people'

Elsewhere, some American voters enraged by Biden's blanket support for Benjamin Netanyahu's war crimes in Palestine are shifting towards Harris after insiders said the vice-president would reduce US military support for Israel by one dollar, on a phased basis, over the next 20 years.

75

# CAUTION

**In the event of a possible victory for Kamala Harris in the US elections, please turn to page 172.**

# DANGER

**In the event of a possible victory for Donald Trump in the US elections, please turn to page 172.**

# ww news

**Waterford Whispers News**

# ENTERTAINMENT

Waterford Whispers News

## CINEMA

# CORK NEVER GOING TO SHUT UP ABOUT THIS

WHILE THERE has been an outpouring of positivity and joy aimed in the direction of Cillian Murphy following his triumph at the Oscars, experts have been quick to warn of the unintended and dire consequences wrought by the awarding of the Best Actor trophy to a Cork man.

'It's set off an Oppenheimer-sized atomic wave of smugness in Cork. Oscar voters might not have realised the horrors they have unleashed but lads in Cork will NEVER shut up about this,' warned one proud Irish man from Waterford, who is all too aware of what this will do to Corkonians.

Undoubtedly it was a great night for anyone involved in the Irish film industry and further proof that this country produces world-class talent out of proportion to its relatively small size; however, Cork natives will never let this achievement go unmentioned in the centuries and millennia ahead.

'They'll be making their own acceptance speeches in their kitchens, in offices, on public transport, like they reared Cillian Murphy and taught him how to act themselves,' said one Irish person fearful of the coming conversations, dry remarks and arrogant proclamations.

'It's not too late for the Academy to reconsider, if there was an Oscar for taking credit for someone else it'd go to Cork, give them that sure but not this, anything but this' shared the Minister for Culture in a statement marking Murphy's win.

'Technically he's lived in England and Dublin longer than he has in Cork, so they've as much claim to him,' offered one desperate Dublin man, in the full knowledge that he has lost this battle.

> 'It's not too late for the Academy to reconsider, if there was an Oscar for taking credit for someone else it'd go to Cork'

### Classifieds

**CILLIAN MURPHY WON AN OSCAR**

This is a weekly reminder that Cillian Murphy won the Best Actor Oscar for his lead role in *Oppenheimer* earlier this year. Cillian is from Cork and is a proud Cork man and we love him so much because Cork is class.

Classified advert financed by the people of Cork.

78

Entertainment

## MUSIC

# TRAGEDY AS MAN USES SHAZAM TO FIND OUT SONG HE'S ENJOYING IS BY JUSTIN BIEBER

ONE MAN's carefully choreographed persona as a fan of only the most refined and unquestionably cool music has made the decision to delete his Shazam app after it informed him the song he was thoroughly enjoying in his local café was in fact by Justin Bieber.

'Never tell anyone about this,' Liam Murphy barked aggressively at the waitress handing the 33-year-old his coffee after she caught sight of his phone screen and the horrors it contained.

With a lo-fi electronic sound reminiscent of the Postal Service, a band Murphy allowed himself to like after first checking they were considered 'cool', 'Ghost' by Bieber lulled Murphy into letting his pretensions fall away and enjoy a song without self-consciously ensuring first that it fit with the image he wants to project to the world of a man of impeccable taste in all things.

'Mad how Shazam acts up and malfunctions all the time, would advise people delete app, something not right,' Murphy followed up in a social media post later that day, covering his tracks.

'Can anyone else see what you Shazamed?' Murphy then quickly Googled, completely dismissing unhelpful suggestions such as, 'hey, it's okay to admit a song by an act you don't normally like is good.'

**2025 Predictions**
Daniel O'Donnell's rap feud with Kendrick Lamar will turn increasingly violent.

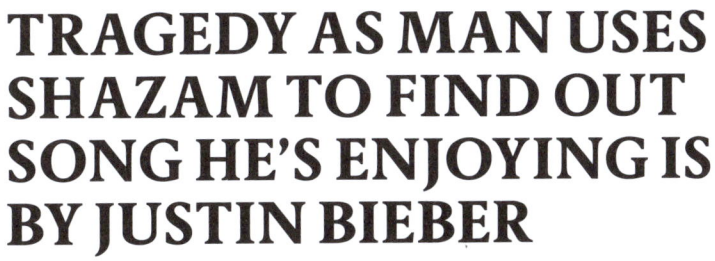

**Mindlessness Tip**
Wow, it's amazing how helpful inspirational quotes are when you're experiencing absolutely no life stress or hardship whatsoever.

# SHATTERING STEREOTYPES: STRAIGHT MAN ATTENDS TAYLOR SWIFT GIG

UPENDING expectations of who a Taylor Swift fan can be, 25-year-old heterosexual man Keith Creggan is broadening narrow minds with his attendance at Taylor Swift's Aviva concerts in Dublin.

'No I'm not going with my girlfriend, mum or sisters,' explained Creggan, who hoped the trailblazing example he sets could see a second and even maybe a third straight man willingly attend a concert by the Eras Tour supremo.

'No it wasn't a ticket I got from an ex-girlfriend that I can't now sell – I just like her music,' retorted Creggan when asked, 'seriously though?'

Creggan has spoken of the suspicion he is greeted with for his out and proud taste in music, which is like heroin to emotionally available women under 35.

'I've asked him, "so this is like a ruse to be in a location where there's loads of angry women looking to get back at their exes and you can be the revenge?", but he's insistent "Shake It Off" is his national anthem,' offered Creggan's still-very-confused-by-all-this friend, Martin Pearson.

UPDATE: Sadly, due to the dangerously high levels of oestrogen present at the gig, Creggan was torn limb from limb during Swift's rendition of 'All Too Well'.

Waterford Whispers News

## TELEVISION

# RTÉ SELL MARTY WHELAN TO LONGFORD WIDOW FOR €3.5M AMID REVENUE DIP

LONGFORD widow Sharon Reilly said she is absolutely chuffed today after securing the purchase of veteran RTÉ broadcaster Marty Whelan in a €3.5m deal with the national broadcaster, *WWN* has learned.

Sold as part of a new revenue-generating model laid out by newly appointed director general Kevin Bakhurst amid a huge dip in licence fees, 67-year-young Whelan will be shipped out of Montrose by courier later this evening to Longford, where he will be put out to stud on Mrs Reilly's country estate.

Bakhurst told *WWN* about his in-house sale. 'Currently, there's also a huge bidding war for Marty Morrisey between a bridge club syndicate from Mayo and an organised sex trafficking gang from Lithuania – it's early days yet but I'm pretty sure we can make up this deficit by the end of the year if we sell off a few more broadcasters.'

Foreign vulture funds are also in negotiations to buy the *Fair City* set and develop the homes in Carrigstown into 200 build-to-rent apartments.

'Unfortunately for Radio 1 listeners, no one wants to buy Ray D'Arcy, so he'll be on the air for a few more years to come,' added Bakhurst.

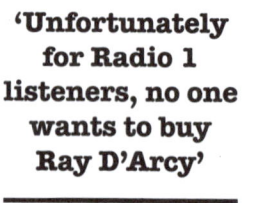

> 'Unfortunately for Radio 1 listeners, no one wants to buy Ray D'Arcy'

**The Year in Numbers**

**1,003** Children conceived to the soundtrack of Daniel O'Donnell's cover of Blackstreet's 'No Diggity'.

---

# ROCKSTAR LEAK: GTA VI CHARACTER WILL BE ABLE TO SNEAK OFF A LITTLE WANK IN THE SHOWER

*grand theft auto VI — COMING 2025*

A REALLY reliable leaker at Rockstar who has never let *WWN* Gaming down before has confirmed that players will be able to sneak off a little wank in the shower during the game, which will in turn bring the character's mental state back down to normal.

'When the character's mental state gets too high, other online players receive rewards for killing them but if you want to avoid being targeted then you'll have to go back to your apartment and crack one off,' said our source.

With rumours abounding as to the details of the highly anticipated sixth edition of the popular video game, Rockstar leak articles have become a click fest for online gaming magazines that generate dozens of articles from even the smallest snippet of information about the game.

'For instance, a *GTA VI* screengrab would be worth more than, say, paparazzi images of Kim Kardashian farting into her cupped hand and then smelling it,' revealed *WWN* Gaming editor Steven Price. 'These fucking nerds will lap up anything we give them whether it's true or not.'

Adding to the latest leak, our Rockstar source also confirmed that *GTA VI* is officially due for release this Sunday evening after dinner behind the shed in your mother-in-law's house at 5.54 p.m., but only if you bring cream buns while wearing wellington boots under a full desert camo burka.

**County Council Notices**

Public information evening on how to lose your shit at the mere sight of a cyclist to take place in town hall at 7 p.m.

Entertainment

## CELEBRITIES

# CELEBRITY WITH UPCOMING ALLEGATIONS? HAVE YOU TRIED SHIFTING TO THE FAR RIGHT FOR SUPPORT?

ARE you a well-known celebrity, politician or person in power who may have abused their position to manipulate, groom, control and assault people for your own sexual gratification? Are you looking for a strategic avenue that will garner support from similar, like-minded people who will literally defend you no matter how heinous a crime you commit? We've got just the playbook for you.

Gently shifting to a far-right conspiracy-based, male-dominated fan base has been proven time and time again as an easy go-to defence mechanism for any narcissistic sexual predator who has preempted a series of 'allegations' against him in the media. You can be far-left too, it's all a horseshoe at the end of the day.

Nicknamed the 'Tate Modern of strategies', suddenly building a follower base of young and impressionable conspiracy-focused males to counteract your sexual violations of impressionable young females is a sure-fire way to create some padding for that upcoming string of investigations and eventual court cases.

As today's social media algorithms reward highly engaging right-wing-based content, rage clicking now represents these platforms' last chance at engagement before inevitably being regulated into oblivion for the greater good of humanity. So why not use this one simple trick to desperately generate support for yourself under the guise of 'they're trying to silence me', or, 'the matrix are coming for me'?

Once you've spent huge sums of money on promoting yourself in videos as an online conspiracy theorist, tell your followers in advance that the big boogeyman will probably one day come for you for simply 'telling it like it is'. This will give the impression that your future arrests are not based on the fact you sexually assaulted dozens of human beings and used them as meat, but instead that it's all down to the New World Order being scared of your social media videos claiming the Jews are a reptilian race trying to implant mind-controlling chips via vaccines.

# Waterford Whispers News

## OPINION

# 'I CAN'T CLIMAX UNLESS SOMEONE SAYS I COULD BE THE NEXT SALLY ROONEY'

*WWN*'s Opinion series gives a voice and platform to people we really shouldn't. This week is the turn of Olwyn Ní Chonaill, a recent prospective applicant for an MPhil in creative writing in Trinity, who is struggling to connect with her sexual partners.

'It's not about the satisfaction of penetrative vs oral sex, foreplay, emotional bonds, all that stuff. No matter how many times I tell sexual partners that I need to hear phrases like "there's a clear intertextual link between Marx and Anne Enright, you're the clear successor to Sally Rooney", then I can't climax.

'We can use all sorts of toys and stimulants, I can be on top or bottom or under the fecking bed, I'm not reaching Nirvana unless someone says "I can see you now with your bangs, in the *Irish Times* opinion pages taking a great big articulate dump on the death throes of capitalism", my legs aren't going to quiver, I'm not going to cum.

'In a time where more and more people are accepting of sexual kinks, I don't think I'm asking much for the lad I met in the kitchen of a gaff party in Ranelagh to say he wants to put his Booker Prize in me, on account of my unique grasp of the ennui brought about by an increasingly interconnected world dominated, paradoxically, by loneliness and isolation.

'I've encountered a shocking amount of judgement with partners too, if they want prostate stimulated, if they need pegging, I am open, I do not shame, but the second I say I can't climax unless they repeatedly tell me they read my transcendental meditation on female intellectuals in an age of fragile masculinity in *The Paris Review*, I'm the weirdo.

'Spanking doesn't really do it for me, but if I'm being spanked while told I've made the Granta best young novelists list then we're going to need a mop.

'Look, for some people it's a simple one-way ticket to heaven via a silent minute-long missionary, but for me it's different, I need people to picture me wearing a turtleneck in the jacket photo of my internationally acclaimed debut novel, and I'm sick of people telling me I need to seek professional help for saying so.'

### 2025 Predictions

In a stunning return to acting, Daniel Day-Lewis wins another Oscar for his portrayal of RTÉ man who slipped on ice in the biopic *My Sore Head*.

Entertainment

## TELEVISION

# RTÉ VIEWERS ALL SAYING SAME THING AFTER DERMOT BANNON TRAPS *ROOM TO IMPROVE* COUPLE IN GLASS PRISON IN HIS BASEMENT

RTÉ'S SMASH hit property show *Room to Improve* produced yet another episode which saw Dermot Bannon's creative input majorly dividing viewers and prompting similar reactions.

Ennis couple Triona and Martin Healy had big plans for their dormer bungalow, which has been in Triona's family for three generations, but not everyone thought Dermot's big ideas were great.

'Surprise, surprise, more window obsession from Dermot,' complained one RTÉ viewer, as Dermot led the Clare couple by gunpoint to a prison cell in a secret basement in his home, which was made entirely of glass.

'I get Dermot's point about "I can see everything, there's no escaping me" but has the man ever had a non-window idea LOL?' asked another viewer.

'What is he like, loves glass everywhere,' said another RTÉ viewer on Instagram showing clips of Triona and Martin begging Bannon to give them some water.

**'Surprise, surprise, more window obsession from Dermot'**

### Mindlessness Tip

Post daily affirmations on Instagram, like 'what's for you won't pass you' to show negative people they only have themselves to blame if they're not happy.

'He gets a fair bit of flak but I love what he's done. When Martin tried to dig an escape tunnel in the corner with his fingernails, the big glass door panel meant Dermot caught him straight away,' shared another viewer, showing not everyone agreed with the criticism.

Waterford Whispers News

## SOCIAL MEDIA

# WE GAVE THIS NEWBORN ACCESS TO TIKTOK, WITHIN MINUTES HE WAS CALLING US 'BLUE-PILLED BETA BOYS'

THERE CAN be little doubt that the algorithms utilised by social media giants such as TikTok and YouTube funnel young and impressionable boys down a rabbit hole filled with brain-in-a-blender wisdom from Andrew Tate and similarly malign influences.

However, *WWN* wasn't satisfied by a new DCU study or an RTÉ investigation, both of which laid bare the realities of young people's exposure to extreme content online.

Fine, we now know that giving a male teenager access to TikTok is the 2024 equivalent of handing over a basket full of dynamite wrapped in copies of *Nuts* and *Zoo* magazines. But the question, 'What happens if you give it to them from birth?' remains dangerously unanswered.

*WWN* takes its responsibilities seriously as a news outlet, and so the obvious next step presented itself; we borrowed our sister's newborn son for the day.

As legally mandated, as an Irish male born in the years 2020–2024 our nephew had to be called Jack. It's fair to speculate that being 23 days old, Jack had yet to form much of an opinion about anything. He was a blank canvas onto which we threw a tin of Dulux paint containing 100% unfiltered TikTok.

As Jack lay in his bouncer, we simply signed him up for an account and let TikTok do the rest.

What happened next was astonishing. He immediately became irritated and cried (a hallmark of misogyny). Next his lip trembled, perhaps because he was annoyed at how he lived in a world where men like him couldn't get a girlfriend. Next, shockingly, the misogynistic brain rot took hold as Jack pursed his lips and stuck out his tongue in search of an imaginary breast.

TikTok had done it. In mere seconds, this little bellicose ball of badness had decided he had a right to a woman's breast. Incredible.

With each minute, TikTok fed him yet another video of an all-male podcast, sigma mindset quote videos, and on and on. Jack cried and cried, such was his anger at a world that so obviously favoured women, who incidentally, according to TikTok, had things called 'body counts'.

Realising the error we had made, we tried to explain to Jack why such content was harmful but it was too late.

'You're just blue-pilled beta NPCs,' Jack scorned.

'Cucktards, that's what you are,' Jack continued, venom pouring from his mouth.

'Women shouldn't be allowed vote, and are merely incubators for my progeny,' Jack said, forcing us to drop to our knees and cry out against our foolish scientific hubris. We had not stopped to think of the consequences, and now the consequences were shouting at us, telling us Hitler actually had some good ideas.

### Community Alert

Mishell is after seaing on Facebook grup der movin migrants into hotell....40,000 of them....there armed with guns....18 foot tall...red eyes....barbed wired mickies on them.

## Entertainment

**MUSIC**

# UNA HEALY STUNS ON RED CARPET LEAVING DOZENS INJURED

JUST when you thought she couldn't stun any more, former Saturdays singer Una Healy stunned on the red carpet over the weekend at the premiere of a new movie, leaving dozens of people injured.

'She's literally stunning,' one eyewitness said as the 42-year-old pulled the trigger of a 50k taser stun gun, leaving one reveller convulsing on the ground behind her as fans screamed for their lives, 'for the love of God someone make her stop!'

Wearing a beautiful skin-coloured dress designed by John Rocha, Una calmly walked over to another unsuspecting man attending the premiere before rendering him 'rigid as an ironing board' as the electricity coursed through his veins before he then keeled over with a loud thud.

'Janey mack, he's like an auld sleeping bullock keeling over after getting pushed,' Una taunted, before turning the taser gun on a spectator trying to escape. 'She's doing the huckle buck beyond, look,' she told horrified eyewitnesses who were now paralysed with fear and cowering from the manic-eyed singer.

After several hours, local emergency crews finally arrived to tend to the victims, many of whom were treated for shock.

'We're not sure we can handle Una being stunning on the red carpet any more, this is the fourth time this week,' one paramedic said, referring to her previous 357 victims so far this year. 'When will this carnage end, when will someone put a stop to her?'

> **Did You Know?**
> The American actor Steve Buscemi thinks he looks perfectly fine.

---

# 9 IN 10 IRISH PEOPLE IN APOCALYPTIC POST-PUNK TRAD BANDS

A RECENT SURVEY estimates that the vast majority of Irish people are now in doom-laden modern trad bands at the vanguard of the alternative music scene, which is the toast of the international music press, *WWN* can reveal.

'At any given time, 9 in 10 Irish people are on a deserted beach or in a hovel of a pub taking moody band pictures,' explained a researcher involved in the survey.

'One man surveyed happened to be tapping on a bin while waiting for a bus only to be given a five star album review in *The Guardian* and "Best New Album" by *Pitchfork*,' added the researcher.

The resurgence in traditional music combined with the eerie, haunting horror you only get when you have the mother of all hangovers is so prevalent that many people wake up in the morning assigned a band and instrument to play.

'It might sound like a fiddle and uilleann pipes being thrown down the stairs for seven minutes straight but it's actually a lament about our lost traditions and common tongue,' explained Eimíle Ní Drisceoil, of the band Smál Dúigh.

'Years ago I would have had these lads here in front of you dancing like eejits on the *Late Late*, but now I have them waffling on about how the collective Irish trauma from the Famine informs their new ska–trad–rap–metal song called 'Them Cunting Brits' in a 10,000-word profile in the *New York Times*,' said Louis Walsh, who, having realised there was money to be made, has put together 49 new trad groups in the last hour.

Sadly this news has seen a 150% increase in the number of lads at parties thinking everybody wants to hear their 3 a.m. rendition of 'Dirty Old Town'.

Waterford Whispers News

## UK ROYALTY
# MEDIA WHO WANTED YOU TO OBSESS OVER WHEREABOUTS OF KATE MIDDLETON NOW WANT YOU OUTRAGED ABOUT SAME THING

'HOW FUCKING dare you, you depraved privacy-ignoring bastards? Leave the poor woman alone,' the tabloid media has lectured for yet another day, as the fallout from Kate Middleton's cancer diagnosis continues.

'No, you're wrong, we didn't lead with thousands of clickbait articles obsessively poring over every detail. We absolutely didn't screenshot and share every batshit insane TikTok deep dives and X threads into Kate's whereabouts in articles, thus helping them spread and flourish. Gaslighting? We've no idea what that is, but we know exactly what "intrusive psycho" means and that's what all of you are,' followed up the tabloids, not getting defensive at all.'

Asking have you no shame, the woman is a mother, the very tabloids who fuelled the invasive furore around the British royal's continued absence from the public have now concluded that anyone who did exactly that deserves a good kicking.

'Shared a meme did you? Life sentences for you, Stephen Colbert and Blake Lively now!' raged the tabloids now trying to coax their gullible readers into participating in a witch hunt against any celebrity who joined in the 'where is Kate?' memeing.

Editors of the rags went on to stress that they reserve the right to do yet another U-turn when one of these public figures receives abusive threats online, at which point they will again act like they had no part to play in such toxic behaviour.

### The Year in Numbers
**9** The number of Sheila McCoughlin's exes who ran in this year's election for right-wing nationalist parties. Jesus, Sheila, you sure know how to pick them.

### County Council Notices
We apologise for the language overheard on a hot mic during an information evening, when a council official was heard to say 'people in tents need our help', these statements do not reflect the opinion of the council. We are sorry if these comments caused you to question your faith in our work.

86

Entertainment

## MUSIC

# MUSIC CRITIC UNDER POLICE PROTECTION AFTER GIVING 9.9/10 REVIEW TO NEW TAYLOR SWIFT ALBUM

A MEMBER of the music press is said to be fearing for their life after becoming the target of threats from Taylor Swift fans on giving the music star's new album a blisteringly negative review.

'Lyrical masterpiece after lyrical masterpiece,' read an extract from the 9.9/10 'hatchet job' review journalist Clara Heller composed for online music publication *Velvet Sounds*, which has so incensed Swifties.

In the wake of Heller's unduly venomous review, which called *The Tortured Poets Department* 'era-defining', armed police have maintained a steady presence outside her apartment and have safely detonated several bombs in controlled explosions.

'I dunno, sort of sounds like to me that she deserves it. Who calls Taylor's production "magisterial, a lush dream brought to life like no one else can" and expects zero backlash?' said one fan wearing a vest with an improvised explosive device on it, who was arrested outside Heller's home earlier this morning.

Police have said a retroactive attempt by *Velvet Sounds* to edit the review and award an additional 0.1 to it only served to further antagonise a rabid sect of Swift's most devout followers.

'I think everyone just needs to take a beat, and let things mellow. Sure, some people will say Clara obviously needs to issue a notes app apology to Swifties, but in practical terms getting surgery to change what she looks like, a new identity and fleeing the country is the easier option,' shared one detective on the scene.

> **'Getting surgery to change what she looks like, a new identity and fleeing the country is the easier option'**

### 2025 Predictions

A nationwide intervention is launched when the '90s hairstyle of a shaved head with long fringe returns.

### Famous Quotes from 2024

"I'm still Jenny from the blockchain"
– **Jennifer Lopez on launching her own crypto currency**

Waterford Whispers News

## TELEVISION

# OBSESSIVE AND DERANGED PERSON TO INTERVIEW REAL-LIFE 'MARTHA' FROM *BABY REINDEER*

THERE ARE fears for the safety of the woman who is the purported inspiration for 'Martha' from Netflix hit *Baby Reindeer* after she agreed to be in the same room as a sycophantic husk of a human being who is known for his obsessive and deranged views and behaviour.

'Someone needs to intervene, this guy has obsessive tendencies; he stalked Meghan Markle for years, constantly posting about her in print and online in some unhinged attempt to get her attention. He's not well,' said one concerned internet user in a comment below a social media post from Piers Morgan announcing his interview with Fiona Harvey.

*Baby Reindeer* has attracted a huge amount of coverage and public interest, with many people seeking out the real identities of people portrayed in the show.

'Oh my God, I couldn't watch it. It gave me nightmares, it's horrible really,' offered one *Baby Reindeer* fan, referring to Piers Morgan's face.

The interview is expected to gain a substantial viewing, thus teaching the media once and for all that exploiting vulnerable people and/or providing a platform to controversial figures for entertainment value will always be rewarded.

'This is a guy who was editor of a newspaper at a time its employees hacked the phones of people, he's not right in the head, he paid people to look through people's bins and take photos of them. This woman is putting her safety at risk,' warned another person.

> 'This woman is putting her safety at risk'

**Famous Quotes from 2024**

"We saved a fortune on make-up due to Irish people's natural, deathly pale complexions"
– Jenna Ortega, on filming season two of Netflix's *Wednesday* in Ireland

## Entertainment

### PORN

# PORN STAR ACHIEVES DREAM OF BECOMING FULL-TIME PLUMBER

A GOOD NEWS story from LA as one of the leading stars in the adult entertainment industry, Wicklow man Glen Dacock, has announced he is leaving the industry to pursue his dream of becoming a plumber.

'I only pursued the porn route because me Ma and Da did it, suppose everyone who had parents that steered them towards a career or industry just because they were in it can sympathise,' explains Dacock.

Well known to your browser's incognito mode, Dacock will now achieve his dream of doing the opposite of what made him famous; unclogging holes.

'If there was ever a script which involved a woman stuck in a washing machine I was all over it, I wanted that part, and on the sly in between takes I'd be checking the bearings on the machine, taking apart pipes under sinks. I just love it,' added the 28-year-old.

'I'll be sad to say goodbye to the friends I've made in the business, but I won't miss the work – repetitive, boring, same thing every day, no thanks. With plumbing every day serves up a new challenge or problem to solve.'

While Dacock admitted his parents were disappointed, his mother Sally's Gap and father Round Wood have grown to accept his choice to enter a field with precarious employment and stiff competition for business.

### MUSIC

# IRELAND REALLY LOVING THIS DYNAMIC PRICING THING

EMBRACING a joyous concept called 'dynamic pricing', ecstatic Oasis fans in Ireland have asked Ticketmaster why they have kept such a brilliant idea from the public for so long.

'It shouldn't be limited to tickets, I'd love for Foodmaster cafe to charge me €800 for a sandwich because I'm fifth in the queue and they heard my stomach grumbling,' said one homeless man *WWN* spoke with.

Oddly, Irish politicians who have 'fuck all' to say about a crisis like homelessness have been very vocal on the matter of dynamic gouging.

'Something is terribly wrong with society if a politician can't glom onto an issue such as this like a bullshit barnacle and claim I'm fighting for everyone. This is why I'm calling for concert tickets to be capped at €5 for everyone,' confirmed every local representative in the country.

Elsewhere, a new Google search term record has been set as people asked 'how do I get a refund on my tickets when Oasis break up?'

UPDATE: Breaking their silence on the fiasco via a short statement, the Gallagher brothers said 'thanks for all your money, cunts'.

Waterford Whispers News

## COSMETIC SURGERY

# ALL THE CELEBRITIES WHO HAVE HAD WORK DONE ACCORDING TO YOUR GIRLFRIEND

SETTLING IN for a night of casual TV viewing can also double up as a chance to enhance your knowledge and widen your education thanks to your girlfriend, who has an encyclopaedic knowledge of celebrity cosmetic procedures.

Here are just some of the latest observations made by your girlfriend in the last 30 seconds as you flicked from programme to programme only to discover every famous person you see has in fact had the following done:

**Selena Gomez** – forehead folding, perma-derma-fillers, kneecap botox.
**Jodie Foster** – nasal scraping, Brazilian butt escalator.
**Ryan Gosling** – nose internship, eye-misting, dimple excavation, internal thermal dermal journal.
**Michelle Keegan** – microwaved ears, big toe shaving, colon bleaching.
**Joe Biden** – wrinkle enhancement.
**Benedict Cumberbatch** – surname abrasion, pectoral shuffle.
**Ariana Grande** – hispanicafication.
**Sarah Snook** – lip emptiers, eyelid deflapping.
**Kieran Culkin** – loin tenderising.

**Denzel Washington** – nothing, the man's perfect.
**Jacob Elordi** – plug draining, de-Australianing.
**Dua Lipa** – cheek explosion, third eye reduction, car freshener armpit scraping.
**Beyoncé** – sock de-clogging, rotator cuff buffering, BBQ thighs.
**Dame Judi Dench** – tits, lips, hips, lipo, you name it.

### Classifieds

**DEADPOOL BUDDY**
Excitable adult man-child seeks fellow baby-man to discuss new Deadpool movie with. Wife will only commit to 30 minutes of my fits of nerdish exuberance. Subjects to be discussed include costumes, Hugh Jackman's biceps, Deadpool quips and surprise cameos.

Entertainment

## TELEVISION

# TDS CONSIDER TRICKING DEE FORBES INTO APPEARING BEFORE OIREACHTAS BY LEAVING BREADCRUMB TRAIL MADE OF FLIP FLOPS

IN A BID to finally get answers from former RTÉ director general Dee Forbes, TDs participating in the Public Accounts Committee have turned to unconventional and morally dubious ways to get the TV executive to appear before them, *WWN* understands.

'Look, we're all out of ideas so it's worth a try,' said one TD, bending down as they made a breadcrumb trail, made of flip flops, starting from outside Forbes's home leading all the way to Leinster House.

The renewed appetite for answers comes as news reports confirmed it turns out the punishment for being the brainchild for wasting €2.2m of the public broadcaster's money on the *Toy Show* musical is being allowed to say you 'resigned' while actually securing a year's worth of salary as a payoff.

'While Ms Forbes wasn't in charge at the time Rory Coveney was punished so lucratively, she could shed light on whether this sort of thing was official policy under her regime,' confirmed another TD, sweating from the effort it takes to line up hundreds of kilometres of flip flops.

'People who work in service of the public, in a broadcasting capacity or otherwise, can't just stonewall TDs like this. She should make herself available for questioning,' added a government TD whose desire for such accountability evaporates the second someone asks about the billion plus overspend on the Children's Hospital.

UPDATE: In disturbing news, some beleaguered RTÉ employees, hitherto uninvolved in the many mismanagement misfires at the broadcaster, have taken to openly burning cash belonging to RTÉ in the hopes they will be punished with an exit package worth €200,000.

# CHARITY APPEAL: FOR JUST €160 A YEAR YOU CAN HELP THIS MAN PAY JOE DUFFY €350K

YOU ARE no doubt aware of the harrowing humanitarian disaster leading the headlines across the world; RTÉ is rapidly running out of money.

You may feel helpless, like there is nothing you as an ordinary person can do, but there is.

For just €160 a year you can ensure RTÉ Joe Duffy's €350,000 salary is paid, but your kind donation does so much more.

Think of how those scared, panicked faces in RTÉ will light up when they realise they can commission another eight glitzy property shows which seem to completely ignore the reality of the ongoing housing crisis, and all because you paid your licence fee.

It has never been so affordable to make a huge difference in the world; with your donation who knows how many existing RTÉ employees can be interviewed yet again on *The Late Late Show*.

The depths of humanity's generosity knows no bottom, and your donation would be further proof of that. Who knows, maybe RTÉ can hire a third Johnny so the other two don't have to work so hard.

Are you honestly saying you wouldn't donate €160 if it meant you never had to see another video of a deeply disturbed man in a car who thinks he is in conversation with the weather?

There are people terrified and traumatised by the fear they will have their car allowance and flip flops taken away from them but you can be the person to make it so this doesn't have to happen.

Don't donate for your own sense of ego, donate for the relative of the RTÉ executive who was hoping RTÉ would still be around to land a cushy number in after they graduate from college.

**Community Alert**

Anyone else think the council installing the pedestrian crossing at the estate's entrance is overkill? That kid barely lost his leg, and what, now we all have to go 20kph out of the estate? Joke!

# Waterford Whispers News

## OPINION

# I CAN'T KEEP UP THE LIE, MY PARENTS THINK I'M IN FONTAINES D.C.

WWN's Opinion series gives a voice and platform to people we really shouldn't. This week it's the turn of failed musician and welfare recipient Ian O'Dowd, who told his parents he was in the band Fontaines D.C.

'Yes, several years ago, in a bid to convince my parents that my decision to make it as a professional musician was not a mistake, I may have insinuated I was in a new band called Fontaines D.C.

'Choosing them for their, at the time, modest success I thought the fact they had a song on the radio would be enough to keep them off my back for another year. However, I had not factored in multiple international tours, Grammy nominations and what I presume is enough money to fuel a debaucherous drug-fueled hedonistic endless party.

'This has all spiralled out of control; if I'm not fielding questions about "Grian and the lads", I'm having to sleep in a tent down a laneway and avoid all face-to-face contact with my parents when the band are out on tour.

'To make sure my parents don't suspect anything I have on several occasions become addicted to drugs, as one presumes rock stars do, I can't do another stint in rehab. Not because I don't want to do drugs, turns out I love them, but there are financial implications for a jobless musician

> 'I'm having to sleep in a tent down a laneway and avoid all face-to-face contact with my parents when the band are out on tour'

who can't accept there isn't a market for a Funk Celtic Rap drummer.

'Hurtfully, my parents bought my excuse that "I was deemed too ugly" to be in any of the posters for gigs or other promotional material.

'I've signed copies of *Dogrel* for all the neighbours. Mam's tennis friends keep asking what the fuck "Starburster" is about.

I need help, and remain open to all remedies to the situation that don't involve coming clean about any of this.'

### Did You Know?
An enormous ice sheet the size of Kanye West's ego has melted away this week in the Arctic ocean.

---

# LOCAL MAN STILL GOING ON ABOUT *DUNE: PART TWO*

DESPITE showing in cinemas for a number of weeks, local man and movie buff Conor Dannon is still going on, at great length, about *Dune: Part Two* and its endless genius, WWN can confirm.

'What do you mean you haven't seen the new *Dune*?' Dannon barked in astonishment at a terminally ill patient at the hospital he works at.

Whether it's discussing the cinematography, the rich world-building, how fucking weird the giant worms are or the acting performances, Dannon's topics of conversation have been stuck on all things *Dune* for some time and show no sign of changing.

'And the sound man, it's like Hans Zimmer himself is giving your ears a rim job or something,' Dannon told cinemagoers in front of him at what was Dannon's seventh screening of the film.

Despite his unvarnished joy and love for Denis Villeneuve's cerebral sci-fi blockbuster, not everyone is appreciative of the 31-year-old's harping on.

'I wouldn't mind him going on about it but he was interrupting my cousin giving the eulogy for my uncle,' said a coworker of Dannon's who has put in a transfer request in a bid to be free of lengthy explanations of how the Fremen could be seen as a stand-in for all oppressed peoples subjected to colonisation.

'Dunno if you know but *Star Wars* borrowed heavily from the original Dune books, and Denis, it's pronounced D'ni, really tried to use practical special effects wherever possible and …' shared Dannon, speaking to his own reflection for what could have been hours.

Entertainment

## DRINKING

# FIVE-EURO PINTS ARE TO LOCAL MAN WHAT BATHWATER IS TO BARRY KEOGHAN IN *SALTBURN*

ONE LOCAL Dublin man has confirmed that his obsessive all-consuming desire for five-euro pints is only comparable to the love Barry Keoghan's character in *Saltburn* showed to some bathwater.

'That slurping sound is universal, man, I'm telling ya. I crave a boozer with the sly fiver pint the way yer man in *Saltburn* loves to consume a bit of jizzy bathwater,' explained pint-haver Jack O'Brien to speechless friends who have now been put off their dinner and all future meals.

Not a common sight in Dublin, O'Brien admits he has to venture outside his home county to have any chance of availing of the now near-mythic five-euro pint.

'Fiver pints are so rare these days, when you see your chance, much like Oliver in *Saltburn*, you've got to take it, go whole hog. Slurp like you've never slurped before, jaysus I'm losing myself just thinking about the creamy five-euro head on those pints, yum,' continued O'Brien, despite everyone within a 10-mile radius begging him to stop.

> **'You've got to leap into that pint like it's a quickly draining bathtub'**

'Don't get me wrong, I'm not aroused by fiver pints but when one of them comes calling you've got to leap into that pint like it's a quickly draining bathtub containing the post-masturbatory watery love juice of the lad you're mildly obsessed with,' added O'Brien, sinking his lips into a freshly poured pint.

Retching friends suppressing their vomit have asked O'Brien why he couldn't just say cheaper pints are nice, like a normal person.

**County Council Notices**

The potholes on Main Street are actually 'traffic calming holes' to stop people driving fast. Genius really.

**Mindlessness Tip**

A great way of reversing a negative tangent of thoughts is by putting two pens up your nose and slamming your face right into the nearest table.

93

Waterford Whispers News

## CELEBRITIES
# MOST FAMOUS PERSON FROM EVERY IRISH COUNTY

A LAND synonymous with trailblazing forces in science, the arts and beyond, Ireland has been the birthplace of many famous people, but just who is your county's most famous person?

**Antrim** – Bobby Sands was born in Newtownabbey.
**Armagh** – Jennifer Lopez, don't be fooled by the rocks that she's got, Jenny said her happiest memories are from when she was shopping in the Halfords at Spires Retail Park and was said to be devastated by its closure.
**Carlow** – Joe Carlow, the cut-price car salesman the county is named after. Carlow's official motto to this day remains, 'There's no low lower than low Joe Carlow's low car prices.'
**Cavan** – Cavan's most famous person is chosen on an annual basis, plucked at random from the county's 76,000-plus population. This year eight-year-old Cormac Fennerton was chosen. Locals have criticised the selection saying, 'I know he's only eight but he's shite.'

**Clare** – Ireland's first dictator Ella Feeney was born in Clare earlier this year. She will take power in a military coup in 2058.
**Cork** – Locals consider Cork the cradle of civilisation, the birthplace of humanity as we know it; therefore, all famous people ultimately come from Cork. But it's Michael Collins. Michael Collins is Cork's most famous person.
**Derry** – Someone connected to the Troubles in some way? Sorry, this writer is from Dublin.
**Donegal** – The real Daniel O'Donnell, the one the current Daniel O'Donnell stole the identity of after killing him in a line-dancing competition that turned violent.
**Down** – Hiace Morrison, the world's best-known Van Morrison tribute act.

**Dublin** – That seagull on O'Connell Bridge that no one fucks with.
**Fermanagh** – John, ah you know John surely, big sad head on him, was caught flashing outside that school in 1981. Peeping John? See, I told you you knew him.
**Galway** – Bob Marley; growing up in Galway, Marley gained a debilitating reliance on weed before introducing it to Jamaica when touring over there.
**Kerry** – Ronán Keane, the inventor of the hard-to-understand Irish accent, originates from Kerry.
**Kildare** – Someone originally from Dublin.
**Kilkenny** – It might sound like a made-up Hollywood tale but Kilkenny is home to DJ and Catriona Carey, a sort of real-life Team Rocket from Pokémon.
**Laois** – 404 famous person not found.
**Leitrim** – Lee Trim, a member of Christopher Columbus's excursions, discovered Leitrim in 1491 after

Entertainment

being tasked with finding the most inhospitable place on Earth. Trim would later lose Leitrim in a card game to a Roscommon farmer.
**Limerick** – Teresa Lynch, the trailblazing Irish woman who invented saying, 'bye bye bye bye bye bye bye' at the end of every phone call.
**Longford** – Center Parcs.
**Louth** – Technically Gerry Adams denies burying Shergar here, but once its grave is discovered it'll be Shergar.
**Mayo** – 149-year-old Cian Ahern, the only remaining Mayo person alive who witnessed the county's last All-Ireland triumph.
**Meath** – Francis Beaufort, who created the Beaufort Scale of Wind Velocities measuring the potency of his farts while at sea in the navy.
**Monaghan** – We have been unable to find anyone willing to admit they are from Monaghan.
**Offaly** – Sadly, Offaly does not have a single famous person.
**Roscommon** – Roscommon lost contact with the outside world in 1983 so it's hard to know who is famous there now.
**Sligo** – The one bearable member of the best three-fifths of the second-best boyband Ireland is known for, *Westlife*, hails from Sligo.
**Tipperary** – Michael Lowry, the famous cult leader, is worshipped like a god in the county.
**Tyrone** – Mickey Harte, legendary GAA coach who despite having a heart for a mickey and a mickey for a heart became an All-Ireland winning coach.
**Waterford** – Mentalist Keith Barry is from Waterford and has dedicated his life to erasing people's minds of this shameful fact.
**Westmeath** – Kim Jong Un, it's here in his native home his radical dislike of Meath was formed, which went on to inform his policies in North Korea when he got the job as leader after applying on LinkedIn.
**Wexford** – Eileen Gray. Who? Expose yourself to some culture, you knuckle-dragging philistines.
**Wicklow** – TikTok sensation Simon Harris has been wowing young people with his epic videos, which parents fear will give children the false impression that you can just fail upwards in life into a well-paying job with zero accountability.

**Community Alert**
Did you hear how much that new couple paid for the McCormack's house? €450,000? This place is a kip!?

## ON THIS DAY

# Waterford Whispers News

VOL 1, 20156136     SATURDAY, NOVEMBER 23, 1963     5p

## Man In Kerry Jersey Spotted At Kennedy Assassination

THEY say you can't go anywhere these days without bumping into someone you know from home, and yesterday's John F. Kennedy assassination was no different when eagle-eyed Irish people spotted a man wearing a GAA jersey in the background.

Paddy Maher from Killarney was seen waving just as the US president was shot through the neck while passing in his motorcade in Dallas yesterday afternoon.

''Twas fair gas; the lads telegrammed me last night sayin' they seen me on the news,' Maher told *WWN* reporters over the telephone this morning, as the image went viral across dozens of Irish newspapers at home, 'I had trainin' with Dallas Ógs at 6 p.m. so I thought nothin' of wearing me GAA jersey beyond, sure I didn't know poor aul President Kennedy would be shot, may God have mercy on him now the poor craytor.'

The son of two had been working in Texas for the past two years and said he would come out to see 'one of Ireland's own' parading through the Dallas streets.

'Jaysis, 'twas some shot in fairness to whoever did it, they didn't leave much of his head intact at all,' Maher recalled of the horrific scene, before confirming he will be a guest on Gay Byrne's new chat show, *The Late Late Show*, next week. 'Sure, I'll have to wear the jersey when I'm on – shame it wasn't under different circumstances, but sure look it, I'll take the fame as it comes, begod.'

Meanwhile, the CIA are still questioning a suspect in the killing and have confirmed they are keeping an open mind, stating this incident could have been a suicide for all they know.

*Continued on Page 2*

## MUSIC

# 'I'VE A FEW PRIESTS ON MY INCOMING LIST ALRIGHT BUT NO BAMBIE THUG', SATAN CONFIRMS

FOLLOWING the backlash online over Ireland's entry choice for Eurovision '24, Bambie Thug, *WWN* travels to the depths of hell to ask are the rumours mainly spread by your terrified Catholic aunt on Facebook true; is Bambi one of Lucifer's very own spawn on Earth?

'Bambie Thug … Bambie Thug … hmmm there's nothing here for the next one thousand years anyway,' the Lord of Darkness told *WWN* while checking his incoming list. We suggested he check Bambie's real name, Cuntry Ray Robinson. 'Nope … I've a Roman Catholic priest by the name of Fr James Robinson from Birmingham alright who's doing 21 years for 21 charges of sexually abusing boys – lenient sentencing even if I do say so myself – but yeah, I've a lot of priests here on the list. I don't know where I'm going to fit them all.'

Confirming our suspicions that the non-binary singer's performance may have just been a camp over-the-top theatrical act developed with one eye on a notoriously camp and over-the-top song contest, Satan suggested that maybe it's the people claiming it was one of his creations who were actually satanically minded as this is exactly the kind of thing he would do.

'I suppose suspicion haunts the guilty,' Satan pointed out, before concluding, 'if a piece of art makes someone so uncomfortable that they question themselves to such a degree that it causes them to act out in a public fashion, then that performance is obviously doing all the right things by bringing the badness out of people – shit always floats to the top.'

> **'I've a lot of priests here on the list. I don't know where I'm going to fit them all'**

### Mindlessness Tip

Start 2025 as you mean to go on; get messy drunk and ring your ex while crying hysterically down the phone.

# ww news

Waterford Whispers News

# LIFESTYLE

Waterford Whispers News

## THE ENVIRONMENT
# DO YOUR BIT TO RECYCLE SO RICH PEOPLE CAN TAKE GUILT-FREE PRIVATE JET FLIGHTS

WITH THE Earth's climate in peril and the fate of future generations at stake it has never been more important to consider what you can do to help rich people take thousands of unnecessary flights on their private jets.

Whether it's sending their staff on a plane a day early to set up the summer house before sending the plane back to pick themselves up, or sending their dog to a pet groomer in Paris, the negative impact the ordinary person has on the environment has never been in sharper focus.

'I'm pretty sure you have to wash out that plastic container before putting it in the green bin,' confirmed a spokesperson for TRPCFRE (The Rich Peoples' Centre For Responsible Excess), an organisation leading the charge to inform the general public on the negative outcomes their daily consumption and recycling habits have on the world.

'Why are you crushing up that can and putting it in a bin in the park? It has the 'R' return symbol on it, c'mon guys, fuck sake,' added the TRPCFRE spokesperson, who should be able to get to New York for their 8 p.m. dinner reservation if the wind is behind them from London.

A survey by the Irish Institute for Climate Change showed a worrying 89% of Irish people don't consider the fact that if they really took to recycling in earnest they could reduce their carbon footprint by 0.003% of that of one private jet flight by an obscenely rich person.

'When you put it like that, I'm ashamed,' said local woman Sharon Boyd, who sometimes chucks the plastic film part of packaging into the recycling even though the instructions state it isn't recyclable.

> 'I'm pretty sure you have to wash out that plastic container before putting it in the green bin'

### Community Alert
Tara Temple from across the way is after losing some weight. Doubt the lazy cow ever went to the gym a day in her life. Ozempic all the way I'd say.

Lifestyle

## SPELLING

# MAN FINALLY SITS HIMSELF DOWN TO LEARN HOW TO SPELL 'ACCOMMODATE'

AFTER booking the day off from work today specially, local man Ger Flynn sat upright in his bed, cracked his knuckles and made his way to his study in the hope of sitting himself down to learn one of his most misspelt words, 'accommodate'.

With the advent of spell correction, Flynn said he's been able to get away with a multitude of words but has decided to face the music and finally go on to wire his spelling neurons correctly.

'It's fine pretending to others you can spell – they don't see the huge number of autocorrects I get flagged on – but deep down there is always that guilt there chipping away at you for not being able to spell a fairly straightforward word,' the 53-year-old public servant revealed.

'There's two fucking m's, Ger, Jesus Christ how hard is it?' Flynn could be heard shouting at himself, now three hours into his study.

'This might take longer than I expected,' he groused, angry with himself for still not being able to spell it, realising now he may not be able to move onto another commonly misspelt word of his after lunch.

'I thought I might get to "definitely" or "colleague" later this afternoon but look, one step at a time,' the English teacher concluded, before booking another two days off work.

### Classifieds
**LONELY HEARTS**

Retiring government TD seeks lucrative consultancy gig with warm and friendly business. I love long walks on the beach and using my knowledge of loopholes in legislation to help you avoid tax, accountability and unnecessary costs.

Deep pockets are essential because I like to be wined and dined.

Waterford Whispers News

## FAMILIES

# STUDY FINDS LOCAL FATHER DIDN'T HAVE IT HALF AS BAD AS HE MAKES OUT

DESPITE his claims to the contrary, one local man has been revealed to be a mammoth fraud after his claims of a life filled with hand-to-mouth hardship has been called into question.

Gerry Turley, most associated by his three children with the phrases 'I had to work for everything I had', 'nothing was handed to me' and 'back in my day', has had his carefully constructed persona as a stoic endurer of hard times obliterated during a family get-together attended by his sister, Catherine.

'Oh that is so Gerry; I seem to remember Mam and Dad paying for you to swan around on a J1 in America. And that's not mentioning the car they bought you when you were back so you could get to your first job, which mam got you 'cus she put in a word with Kavanagh Motors for you,' offered Catherine, in response to Gerry remonstrating with his children once again over their perceived fecklessness and privilege.

The 58-year-old is believed to be one of just 79,000 Irish fathers who completely erase all memories and knowledge of all the leg-ups they received in life just so they can play the role of stern, pulled-myself-up-by-my-bootstraps lone wolf.

'And he dropped out of his arts degree – bet he never told you that,' added Catherine, prompting Gerry to clutch at his heart as his world shattered around him, the high ground he had maintained in all lectures to his children fading beneath his feet.

### County Council Notices

Buskers: all Ed Sheeran songs carry a €500 fine with a minimum five-year prison sentence so please don't fucking test us – we'll throw away the bloody keys if we have to.

Lifestyle

## DRUGS

# MAN WANTS SAME PRAISE FOR NEVER TAKING DRUGS THAT PEOPLE GET FOR GIVING THEM UP

A STRAIT-laced local man who was always too fearful of his parents' wrath and riddled with anxiety to ever attempt drug taking of any kind has called for an overhaul in how society approaches commending and supporting those who overcame their drug addictions.

'I'm all for supporting people but while you're all handing out congratulations and fair plays, do you know when the last time I had cocaine was? Never,' offered Waterford native Tiernan Shanley.

Courageously breaking what he considers a major taboo, Shanley suggests he should also get one of those sobriety chips on account of 35 years of being drug free.

'The fact I was born 35 years ago and haven't ever touched any substances to begin with shouldn't bar me from getting even a small bit of praise,' added Shanley, who has been warned that lingering outside Narcotics Anonymous meetings and gloating about his 35 years is a tad irritating.

Brought to tears by the solidarity and pride people express in those who have been able overcome addiction, Shanley simply wants recognition.

'No book publisher would be interested in my memoir, there's been no low point, no coming back from the brink, so I think it wouldn't kill some people to give me a pat on the back for that,' Shanley outlined.

'I mean it's great you're not stealing your little brother's communion money any more to settle a debt with a dealer but some of us were robbed of those milestones because we thought our eyeballs would explode if they came into contact with secondhand spliff smoke. Being this boring takes bravery and courage too, I take it one day at a time as well.'

## SOCIAL MEDIA

### PUBLIC REMINDED TO ONLY TRUST RANDOM SOCIAL MEDIA ACCOUNTS FOR FACTUAL INFORMATION ON ISRAEL/HAMAS CONFLICT

TO AVOID unnecessary use of common sense and critical thinking, the public has today been reminded to seek out random social media accounts in the search for accurate information.

'If you feel like NuttyCatPics27 isn't random enough of a social media account, don't worry, a friend will be along to send a video from an account called خيالي or RyanReynoldsFeetFanClub and from there just blindly believe everything,' experts urged as they sought to help people gain a greater understanding of an unfolding crisis.

Social media users have also been told to just go ahead and implicitly trust screenshots that carry the logo of a legitimate news outlet even if the headline reads 'Swifties Infiltrate Hezbollah, Behead Leadership Before Screaming Taylor Swift Akbar'.

'Do not, and we repeat, do not accept that the seconds directly after an alleged attack/explosion/invasion/shooting might not be when a full, accurate picture of events can be discerned. Just jump on social media, believe the first disturbing and emotive thing you see, and then jump in the comment sections to stir shit up. These are the foundations on which we can build peace in the 21st century,' added another expert, annoyed by imbeciles who choose to wait for further information on things.

'And when you read "Hamas claims" or "IDF claims", immediately do that thing in your brain where you label a media outlet "liars" for informing you that they are merely reporting on the fact an entity has given their side of the story or version of events,' they concluded, happy that WhatsApp groups everywhere were receiving at least a dozen 'dunno if real but looks legit' videos every 30 seconds.

101

Waterford Whispers News

## BARBECUES

# LADS SHOULD GET AT LEAST 2 HOURS' SMALL TALK OUT OF MAN'S PURCHASE OF NEW BBQ

A GROUP of men are celebrating the fact that one of their crew has purchased a new BBQ, removing all need for their conversations to dig beneath the surface and involve sharing their foremost concerns, worries and problems.

'Some sizzle off that I'd say,' offered one man, delighted to be able to talk endlessly about friend Rob Tynan's purchase of a Weber Spirit E323s GBS.

'Is it good with the gas, yeah? Doesn't use up too much?' offered another man who feared being dragged to Rob's BBQ could result in him having to emote feelings and address the fact his wife recently left him.

Marvelling at Rob's admission that his wife nearly didn't let him get it when she learned of the €900 price tag, the men were able to cling on to questions about the warranty and whether Rob will leave it out on the patio or put it back into the shed after every use.

'How much? Fuck me, ah no in fairness, it'll earn it back. Some spread you have going in fairness, yeah, did it come with the tongs?' offered another man, who usually dreaded these occasions due to his lack of sports knowledge greatly hindering his ability to talk about anything except his life.

The men rejoiced once more and thanked the gods for the brand new BBQ as Cormac, a man they know nothing about and can't gel with no matter how hard they try, joined the group and exclaimed, 'now that Weber is a serious bit of kit!' in favour of talking about his recent cancer diagnosis.

> **Community Alert**
>
> Not naming names but SOMEONE should rein their kids in because SOMEONE, not naming names, clearly can't control them and their violent tendencies. One more incident of SOMEONE's child punching my girl on the arm will see them reported to Tusla. Mairead, you're a terrible mother and you've been warned.

## RELATIONSHIPS

# HOVERING OVER YOUR MISSUS WHILE SHE'S GETTING READY SPEEDS UP PROCESS BY 300%, FINDS STUDY

A NEW study carried out by John from Urlingford has found that if you hover over your partner while they're getting ready to go out somewhere with you it can speed up the process by 300%.

Standing impatiently with your jacket on and an annoyed expression on your face was found to be the best course of action to speeding up the application of make-up, doing hair and choosing the perfect outfit, John found.

'Sighing loudly also works,' the lone researcher published in his report. 'Staring at her reflection in the mirror like you're about to murder someone is another trick I like to use, or pacing up and down the hall and jingling your keys – man, I'm a professional at this craic.'

> **'Staring at her reflection in the mirror like you're about to murder someone is another trick I like to use'**

John, who has since become single after publishing his findings, added that waiting in the car outside and revving the engine every so often is also a great way of ending a relationship if needed, stating that he will publish a book on his research later next year.

'I'm going to devote an entire chapter on how to give women the ick,' the full-time son of two added. 'I'll teach men how to perfect that annoying high-pitched baby voice and show them how revealing your own insecurities by using jealous remarks can relieve you of being held back by the old ball and Jane… I mean chain.' He added, 'oh, God, I'm sorry, Jane, I love you – please text me back.'

### 2025 Predictions
Some of your mad uncle's conspiracy theories are actually proven true.

### Mindlessness Tip
Listen to your gut. 'Grrrraaghgapufffpliipgh' is pretty good advice.

Waterford Whispers News

## ASTROLOGY

# 'OH, I'M AN ARIES' SAYS WOMAN UNDER IMPRESSION IT EXCUSES HER SHITTY BEHAVIOUR

RELATIONSHIP experts have once again been forced to issue a reminder that invoking your star sign is not a one-size-fits-all excuse for shitty behaviour, following one local woman's increased deployment of the phrase 'Oh, I'm an Aries' every time she offends someone.

'Sorry, I'm an Aries; that's just sort of how we are, can't help it,' said Ciara Taffin of some awful behaviour she absolutely didn't have to subject a loved one to.

Insulting people's appearance, deliberately half-assing her job, refusing to help friends or family with anything, repeatedly cheating on her boyfriend – just some of the things Taffin has in the last week put down to the unstoppable force of her 'Ariesness'.

'You're saying it like there's something I can do about it, I can't, it's the Aries in me,' Taffin said, eating her six-year-old niece's last square of chocolate.

Experts have asked that, if people are looking for get-out-of-jail-free cards for their intentionally obstinate, arrogant and poisonous ways, they try blaming it on being from Cork instead, as that's a more rooted-in-science explanation.

'You're giving off big Taurus energy, my guy, back off,' Taffin later declared to a guard who seemed to think being an Aries wasn't a satisfactory explanation for why she was driving under the influence the wrong way up the M50.

### Famous Quotes from 2024

"It's an honour to be your boyfriend's most googled (in incognito mode) search term"
- Sydney Sweeney, on her growing fame

## SELF-CARE

# MAN GROWS BEARD AS APOLOGY TO SELF FOR NOT HAVING HAIR ON HEAD

IN A BID to curry favour with the vacant retail space above his eyebrows a man who recently went bald has decided to grow a beard, in a bid to cheer up his cold, barren noggin.

'It's my way of saying don't worry, we've still got something going on, y'know?' said Waterford man Simon Ruane.

'There is a small percentage of me which is trying to trick my follicles to the point where my sideburns just keep growing upwards like ivy or something,' added Ruane.

The 34-year-old was left with no alternative but to shave his head after realising if he held out any longer he'd be living a farcical lie which would involve a combover.

'I didn't want to do it, I know you're mad but look what's going on down here, we've got something going on, it's a chin party and everybody's invited,' Ruane reasoned with his now bald dome.

'No, don't be silly no one is even going to notice, not with this show-stopper decorating my chin like an ornate ginger Aran jumper,' Ruane continued to reassure his head.

Lifestyle

EXCLUSIVE

# LOCAL MAN GOING THROUGH WHOLE-LIFE CRISIS

FINALLY diagnosed after 44 years, local man Tommy Rotchford breathed a sigh of relief today after being diagnosed with what doctors are calling a 'whole-life crisis', WWN has learned.

After spending decades wondering why nothing ever goes his way, Rotchford said he now accepts his condition and can hopefully move on with his train wreck of a life.

'All I needed was someone to confirm that yes, I was doomed from the second the doctors used a forceps to rip me from my mother's womb,' the son of two said. 'If it's not health issues, it's relationship issues; I never have money and seem to be always trying to recuperate from one setback after another – finally I realise now that I'm going through a whole-life crisis.'

Much like a midlife crisis, when a person of middle age begins to question the things that they have accomplished or achieved and whether those same things still provide a sense of fulfilment and meaning, a whole-life crisis is a constant period in a person's life where they realise this entire shitshow is one big uphill struggle laden with obstacles designed to rip every fibre of your soul into a million tiny pieces so that by the end of it you're left with nothing but hate and contempt for your fellow man and planet.

'Yup, that's me alright,' Rotchford proudly took the news. 'Fucking nailed it.'

Since his diagnosis, the Waterford man has reported a new lease of life after realising that once you're at the very bottom, there is only one way left to go.

**County Council Notices**

Road works on the quays will take place Monday to Friday at peak times in a bid to disrupt as many commuters as possible. We're not sorry for any inconvenience – we love this shit.

105

**Waterford Whispers News**

## FAMILIES

# HAS A FRIEND STATED THEY DON'T WANT CHILDREN? HERE ARE 10 DIFFERENT WAYS TO TELL THEM THEY ACTUALLY DO

NO MATTER HOW explicit the message is, regardless of its clarity and regular repetition, when a friend says they do not and will not have children, there's only one thing for it: insist they do in fact want children and are mistaken.

Here are the 10 best and most condescending ways you can inform a friend or loved one of this.

1. 'Never say never.'
2. 'Being a parent is the most important thing you'll do with your life, you'll see.'
3. 'Ah yeah, but you'll change your mind.'
4. 'You'll change your tune when you meet someone. Emily, stop pulling your sister's hair or so help me. Honestly, she's like the demon offspring from a horror movie sometimes haha.'
5. 'Ha, I said the same thing but sure didn't I have three in the end. A holiday? No, we've been broke for 18 years.'
6. 'You say that now but just you wait. Micheal, get down off that. Jesus, he's thick as his father. Dimmer than a cinema.'
7. 'But what will you do when you're old and need someone to take care of you? Jamie, where are you going? You're grounded after last week's little stunt. Don't you call me a bitch, can't you see we have guests!'
8. 'You're young but when you mature you will want them. Colm, put that down now, it's a knife not a toy! They broke the mould when they made him, smashed the mould to pieces because they knew they'd made a mistake.'
9. 'The dog is the trial run I'd say, is it? Ah no you'll love it when you do eventually have them. Stephen, what have we said about shitting on the kitchen floor? Potty training this little prick for a year now at this stage. Arse on him like a diarrhoea canon.'
10. 'Usually when a couple say they don't want kids the woman really does want them, that's probably the same with yourselves? Oh don't mind me crying, I just get like this anytime I'm overwhelmed which is always lol.'

Lifestyle

## SHOPPING
# THINGS YOU SHOULDN'T SAY WHEN IN A SEX SHOP

CROSSING THE threshold of an establishment such as a sex shop can invoke nervousness in many people. *WWN* is here to help you through your journey with a list of phrases to be avoided there in a bid to minimise awkwardness.

- 'Where are your dressing rooms? I'd like to try this on. Yes, I know it's a dildo.'
- 'Can you gift wrap that, it's for my daughter.'
- 'Do gimp masks work on kidnap victims just the same?'
- 'What's your returns policy? I got this five years ago and the rechargeable battery is kaput.'
- 'Do you do casting moulds of penises? Of course I have mine out, how else are you going to mould it?'
- 'I've been a very, very well-behaved boy so I'm looking for a sheet of stickers, maybe with gold stars on them.'
- 'I'm here to return something. I have the receipt and yes, technically speaking, I have it with me, there's just one problem.'
- 'I know you stock Ann Summers but do you have any Stormy Winters?'
- 'One anatomically correct Donald Trump sex doll please.'
- 'The rampant rabbit doesn't do it for me any more, I'm going to need a relentless rhinoceros.'
- 'You call these nipple clamps? I had to use 12 of them on one of my tits just to get the slightest hit!'
- 'Do you want any of my old school uniforms to sell on?'

### Famous Quotes from 2024
"Whatever you do, don't put 'an end of an era', or 'closes its doors' into Google Ireland"
- Paschal Donohue

### Classifieds
**COMPLAINT**
Not looking to buy/sell anything but just wanted to let everyone know that myself and my husband Derek had a meal in Reilly's Fish Restaurant on Main Street last night and they never bothered to ask me if my food was okay. Very bad customer service. I said posting this in the classifieds section of the local newspaper was a far better way of getting my point across rather than actually saying it to the restaurant themselves at the time. Shame as the food was absolutely bloody amazing.

Mary

## SHOPPING

# NOTHING COMPARES TO WAVE OF PEACE THAT CRASHES OVER LOCAL FATHER WHEN HE'S BROWSING WOODIES

WATERFORD FATHER Noel Power has credited his local DIY emporium with delivering him a rare sense of calm that eludes even the greatest practitioners of Zen meditation.

'I can't explain it, but when I'm searching for the right drill bit it's total Nirvana,' explained Power, who remains a constant source of negative grousing within his own home but is transformed when browsing Woodies.

Power acknowledged the fact that he could probably find whatever item he's looking for within seconds if he asked staff for help, but prefers to aimlessly walk the aisles for upwards of two hours.

'And to think some eejits spend thousands on retreats at the foothills of the Himalayas for the sort of peace I achieve every weekend off the Cork Road,' said Power, now running his hands over BBQ set after BBQ set and testing out the comfort of 84 different outdoor chairs.

Only once his initial browsing is finished does Power enter a higher plane of being by finally engaging staff and grilling them about the technical aspects of sanders, halogen heaters, trailing sockets and radiator covers.

> 'And to think some eejits spend thousands on retreats at the foothills of the Himalayas for the sort of peace I achieve every weekend'

'Troubles? What troubles, I've just spent 18 minutes learning about the Bosch Cordless Chainsaw 18v,' added Power who then took his final serene form by guffawing repeatedly in a dismissive fashion at the news that the chainsaw has a 79-minute charge time.

Power's tranquil demeanour has led to a growing number of yogi masters traveling from India and turning up to the Woodies branch in search of self-actualisation.

**County Council Notices**

Apologies, we didn't think through holding the information evening on disability awareness week on the fourth floor in a building with no elevator.

## SOCIALISING

# '6 A.M. CLOSING TIMES COULD MEAN YOUNG PEOPLE MIGHT ENJOY THEMSELVES' WARN TDS

FINE GAEL TDs have urged taoiseach-in-waiting Simon Harris to scrap the nonsense late licensing law legislation aimed at growing the night-time economy due to the fact that it could give young people a chance to enjoy themselves.

'It sends the wrong message, young people exist solely as an economic force to be moulded and exploited for profit, to suggest they have free time they can use to socialise is terrifying,' shared one TD who has decided that adopting the 'contrary old bollocks' persona gives him his best chance at being re-elected.

> 'It sends the wrong message, young people exist solely as an economic force to be moulded and exploited for profit'

The implementation of 6 a.m. closing times had been promised by the coalition government sometime before humanity adopted the Gregorian calendar and is set to be delayed once more after TDs rightly highlighted the fact that young people in Ireland are only allowed to do two things: suffer and emigrate.

'I can see it now, toddlers doing heroin in a dance clubbing emporium,' shared one Fine Gael TD mid-fainting.

'What's worse, some people will open venues to cater to dancing and congregating, and create jobs, providing tax revenue to the Exchequer. It's the stuff of nightmares.'

Fine Gael TDs went one step further in pointing out that every young person they speak to is against the idea of having more places to socialise and instead is begging the party to get on with the important work of blaming Sinn Féin for everything.

### Mindlessness Tip
Share cryptic posts about something awful having happened to you on social media so people will give you some attention.

### 2025 Predictions
Your mother will continue in her struggle to say Dua Lipa correctly.

Waterford Whispers News

## SOCIAL MEDIA

# 'GO WOKE, GO BROKE' WRITES UNEMPLOYED 37-YEAR-OLD BACHELOR STILL LIVING AT HOME WITH PARENTS

NESTLED in his PlayStation gaming chair that his parents bought him for his 39th birthday, Waterford bachelor Martin Kehoe smugly cast his eye over his latest X post with the sort of satisfaction normally the reserve of a poet who has completed his magnum opus.

'Go woke, go broke,' Kehoe replied to a news article detailing the closure of a local gay-friendly nightclub due to the ongoing cost-of-living crisis. 'Serves them right for falling into that shite,' he added of the closure, which led to the club's 25 staff being made redundant.

Scratching off gum stains from the crotch of his ill-fitting cotton tracksuit pants he bought in Penneys in 2011, Kehoe refreshed his X feed in the hope of some leftie taking the bait, only to realise he had yet again been lumped into the 'See More Replies' section.

'They're shadow-banning me again!' the full-time son of two exclaimed, now even more furious at the world that left him behind post-Leaving Cert. 'They did the same thing to my "burn it down" reply last week on that hotel announcement about refugees. I'm going to tag Elon Musk now, it's obviously some bot glitch, cause Elon isn't like that at all, Elon would retweet me if he saw it.'

> **'I'm going to tag Elon Musk now, it's obviously some bot glitch, cause Elon isn't like that at all, Elon would retweet me'**

Realising *Pawn Stars* was starting in five minutes, Kehoe saw he would have to multi-task being an asshole online alongside watching his favourite day-time TV show.

'Mam! Can you make me some lunch, there's someone wrong here on the internet and I need to spend the next couple of hours bombarding them with tweets until they block me, thanks,' he shouted, before sneaking off for his habitual pre-*Pawn Stars* wank.

### Community Alert

Guys, can we all agree that leaving bikes and the like on the green is very 'social housing'. Let's put a stop to it before Sinn Féin councillors start appearing like flies on shit thinking they'd get our votes.

# Lifestyle

## DINING

# 'STOP KEBAB SHAMING' – DRUNK PEOPLE CALL FOR DIGNITY WHEN HORSING INTO MESSY MEAT POCKETS

THE nation's kebab munchers have called on the people of Ireland to respect their dignity when horsing into their favourite messy meat pockets on the street post-session, stating that 'kebab shaming' needs to stop if we want to move on as a society.

Sick of being looked down upon by more sober revellers on nights out, kebab enthusiasts are now calling on the Government to include kebab shaming in any new proposed privacy laws in a bid to protect munchie-ridden soakagers.

'Yeah, there's garlic mayo and chilli sauce all over my face, so what? It's the dog's bollocks, okay?' barked campaigner Mark O'Dwyer who was demonstrating the ongoing 'foodism' outside his favourite kebab shop in Waterford at 2am last Sunday morning after drinking his own weight in booze. 'You can't eat these things without making a mess sober, so what chances do we have drunk? It's not fair,' he added, before succumbing to a chronic bout of hiccups and falling into a taxi home.

'People filming and sharing videos online of drunken people engaging in the intimate act of kebab defiling should be jailed,' shared one kebab enthusiast.

However, those opposed to public displays of kebabbing (PDK) have retaliated against the calls to scrap kebab shaming, claiming people have the right to stare at and judge other people for their sloppiness and for leaving bits of lettuce and onion everywhere on the street with a head on them like a burst purple cabbage.

'Over 500 people are killed every year in Ireland from slipping on kebab bits,' a spokesman for Anti-Kebab Munchers Ireland said. 'A further 300,000 taxis are soiled every year, costing millions of euros in damage. How much longer do we have to stand aside and ignore this epidemic? These people are monsters; they're the lowest of the low.'

## FAMILIES

# A PARENT'S WORST NIGHTMARE: THE CULCHIE BOYFRIEND

YOU CAN work hard at raising your children right, but for city dwellers and townies everywhere there is a scenario they fear more than anything when it comes to their kids: the day they bring a culchie home.

Such a nightmare scenario has engulfed one suburban home in a leafy Dublin area where parents John and Fiona McAniff have been informed by their youngest daughter Ciara that she has taken up with a young man from a rural backwater.

'The language will be a big adjustment for him, have you considered that, Ciara?' bleated Fiona, already catastrophising.

Ciara reminded her parents that her Longford-hailing boyfriend Martin McCreedy does in fact speak English, and that stereotypes can be both hurtful and unhelpful.

'Have you thought this through, Ciara, have you taught him how to use the Luas? You know I heard of a culchie who fell down the gap between a Dart and the platform and that was the end of him. You'll be like a full-time culchie carer,' continued Fiona, failing to hear Ciara inform her that Martin has lived in Dublin for eight years.

Finding no delicate way to phrase it, Ciara's parents explicitly stated that McCreedy's family had a completely different culture and value set and weren't necessarily compatible with civil city life.

'We've never been a coleslaw household, as you know well, and he can't expect bacon and cabbage every time he's over. We only get the *Sunday Times* of a weekend, I don't think we get the *Farmers Journal* in Dublin, Ciara. Ciara!' Fiona added, while John wisely stayed out of the line of fire.

'What's your poor dad going to talk to him about? He knows f-all about fertiliser and slurry. He's never watched the *Late Late Country Special* either! Honestly, Ciara, would you get back with Jamie?' Fiona said, in a reference to Ciara's last boyfriend, who dumped her after turning cheating into an Olympic sport.

Waterford Whispers News

## EMIGRATION
# YOUNG IRISH PEOPLE EXPLAIN WHY THEY MOVED ABROAD

**WHILE EMIGRATION** is a huge part of the nation's history, no two experiences are the same. *WWN* spoke to some ex-pats who revealed the reasons they felt the need to move abroad.

'I have a better chance of catching chlamydia off Ryan Gosling and Margot Robbie during a threesome than I do of paying reasonable rent in Dublin so …'
– **Sean O'Neill, now living in Glasgow**

'Like I'm going to just list my outstanding warrants back in Ireland to a random stranger, fuck off with ya!'
– **Ciara Hurley, now on the run in Dunedin**

'When I was younger I had a cousin who moved to Australia and on visits home he used to spend the whole time talking about how crap Ireland was, and how everything here was done wrong and that they do it much better abroad, and I thought to myself; I want to be that annoying when I'm older so I moved abroad there last year after finishing college.'
– **Lisa Fanton, now in Perth**

'There's currently no extradition treaty between Ireland and the UAE.'
– **Daniel Kinahan, now in Dubai**

'It was a big culture shock but you get used to it after a while. The locals aren't the most welcoming but you can't have everything.'
– **Eabha Preston, now living in Cork**

'I always wanted to be in the army but the Irish Army is neutral and would be seeing no action so it seemed a no-brainer to go abroad.'
– **David O'Brien, member of Iran's Islamic Revolutionary Guard Corps**

'I don't want to raise my hypothetical children in a cloistered, small-minded backwater of a town which trades in begrudgery and intolerance, so I had to leave for the complete opposite.'
– **Paula Power, now living in Florida**

'Since I was a child I had always dreamed of being that random lad in a Kerry jersey at a big international sporting event, but that's not possible sitting on my arse at home so off I went.'
– **John Cassidy, now in Las Vegas**

'There's better pay and job opportunities in my chosen field in Saudi Arabia so the choice was sort of made for me.'
– **Martin Borden, executioner in Saudi Arabia**

Lifestyle

## SHOPPING
# LOCAL MAN NEVER KNOWS WHICH BIN BAGS TO BUY

INSPECTING the large selection of various bin liners in his local supermarket, local man Ben Reeves admits he never really knows exactly which bastarding bin liners to buy, WWN reports.

Trying to recall the texture, colour and size of that one perfect roll of rubbish sacks he bought over two years ago, Reeves cursed the large variety of 'flimsy auld shite' currently on display.

'This one now was durable and fitted the bins at home like a pair of slip-on Sketchers,' the dad-of-two told a confused teenage shop assistant, who just wished the ground would open and swallow one of them up. 'Not this crap now that doesn't rip when you part it from the roll,' Reeves demonstrated, holding up one of those white plastic rolls that wouldn't fit a sand bucket.

Stuck with over 20 different versions under his sink at home, the 38-year-old vowed to take a stand and to never waste money on crap bin liners again.

'What size? Fucking bin size, whatever the fuck the size of a family bin is,' he barked at some ridiculous question about size. 'Am

> '**Am I meant to measure the volume now too – it's a family bin in the kitchen – that size!**'

I meant to measure the volume now too – it's a family bin in the kitchen – that size!'

With the situation escalating, two security men were now tasked with intervening on aisle 4 as Reeves suggested borrowing one of each roll, testing them at home to see which one it is he wants before dropping the other ones back later.

'Get off me, I just want the right fucking bin liner, you Nazis!' he pleaded as the men restrained him on the ground until the gardaí arrived.

**2025 Predictions**
Human brain cells are officially added to the endangered species list.

## Waterford Whispers News

**DRUGS**

# BABY CRYSTAL'S CHRISTENING, GER'S RETIREMENT DO: THE FULL LIST OF EVENTS AFFECTED BY €157M COCAINE SEIZURE

THE LIST of events that have been tragically altered by the seizure of €157m of cocaine off the Irish coast is growing by the minute.

The IAS (Irish Association of Sessions) now has a full list of events affected and has advised attendees to make the necessary precautions and alterations to plans, which mainly include not bothering to turn up.

### The Year in Numbers

**8** The number of orgies taking place in every Irish household, as that can be the only reason gonorrhea cases have risen in Ireland by 67%.

The events include:

- The parents of little Crystal Casey are devastated to report the christening of their child will no longer involve 'a mad one'. Similar notices have been filed by the parents of Joshua Heaney O'Driscoll, Rainbow Brennan, Chloe, Joey & Zoe Byrne, Tarquin Shaftesbury and Beyonce Fennessy.
- Ger Kelly's retirement do from Carew Medical Devices has been cancelled until the next shipment makes it through without being detected.
- Teacher training day during upcoming midterm at St Denis' Of The Deviated Septum will be much more boring.
- The Citizens' Assembly on Drugs.
- Sheila Martin's OAP book club and knitting circle's monthly meet up.
- 15,403 different house parties too great in number to list individually.
- Any gathering in excess of two people that involves any estate agents, solicitors, doctors, artists, marketing professionals and so on.
- All pub toilets.
- One event which is being brought forward and expanded is the Garda Christmas party in Cork.
- Wexford beach clean-ups this weekend now have a record number of volunteers offering to comb the coastline for rubbish which could have run aground.

Lifestyle

## RELATIONSHIPS

# WOMAN JUST GOING TO GO THROUGH BOYFRIEND'S PHONE THIS ONCE, SHOULD SOLVE TRUST ISSUES FOREVER

ANY LINGERING paranoia which exists in one Dublin woman's mind and fuels her trust issues and insecurities will all but be eradicated if she just gets this one good nosy through her boyfriend's phone, *WWN* can reveal.

Emma Sheehan (26) has gone on record with friends to state that her boyfriend Tom Boggins was foolish enough to let her observe his phone's PIN code, giving her the perfect opportunity to confirm if her paranoid delusions based on nothing are true, and if not that'll be that.

'We've been going out for three years, he's my own personal lap dog, has no hobbies or social life outside of me, so naturally I think maybe, just maybe, he's having an affair at work with his 57-year-old manager Margaret. Why else would he have mentioned her in passing once seven months ago,' reasoned Sheehan, reasonably.

> 'We've been going out for three years, he's my own personal lap dog, has no hobbies or social life outside of me'

The genius of Sheehan's plot to access Boggins's phone and trawl through it is that it's the only way to finally silence her doubts and put them to bed once and for all.

'Like girls, you know me, if I see no dodgy texts, it's not like I'm going to find something suspicious in him following a girl on Instagram I've never heard of, who is in fact his cousin. I'd never let something like this blow up in my face,' Sheehan said to friends, who enthusiastically encouraged her spiralling like it was a sensible line of inquiry.

'Who the fuck is this bitch,' added Sheehan of her boyfriend's contact list, which included a woman called 'Mam'.

### Did You Know?
The people of Cork are the only ancient, uncivilised tribe to worship themselves as their own God.

**Waterford Whispers News**

## CULCHIES

# 'IT'S LIKE CULCHIE CHRISTMAS': HOW TO EXPLAIN THE PLOUGHING CHAMPIONSHIPS TO A DUB

SCENES of families being buried in a muddy grave in a car park in Laois aside, the Ploughing Championships represent the pinnacle of culchie culture and the most enjoyable experience on Planet Farming.

However, it's still a struggle for urban Dubs to comprehend such things. To help Dubliners better understand the unique draw of the championships, WWN asked attendees to explain it in terms them up in Dublin would understand.

'For a culchie, watching competitive ploughing is a serene contentment few of us will ever know but it's basically the same thrill vegans would get from watching the Happy Pear wrestle in a paddling pool of organic fair trade jelly.

'It's like the Brown Thomas Stephen's Day sales but for lads buying Massey Fergusons. It's culchie Christmas, well an additional culchie Christmas to actual culchie Christmas. And FYI, the Rose of Tralee is basically our New Year's Eve and any Garth Brooks gig is Halloween.

'It's the Taylor Swift Eras tour but instead of crowds of screaming young women unable to control themselves, there's a crowd of lads in Ben Sherman shirts attending a cow insemination seminar, it's somehow wildly different but the same.

'Look, you don't have to "get" it, culchies don't get why Dubs all have the same haircut, wear Canada Goose like it's a uniform or talk in a whiny high pitch frequency only dogs can hear.

'You know how you and your hipster mates react to a new craft beer? Well, imagine 80 craft beer festivals happening at once and it's just as much a meat market as Harcourt Street at 2 a.m.

'It's like a horror movie in which everywhere you turn there's thousands of Two Johnnies.'

---

# 'WHO'S LAUGHING NOW?' DVD COLLECTOR SELLS ENTIRE COLLECTION FOR €75

'THEY all called me mad, but the only people mad now are the losers who lost out,' DVD collector Tony Fielding gloated today after securing a deal with a local pawn shop for a staggering €75.

Starting his collection in the late '90s, Fielding scoured video stores around the country for the best bargains, accumulating more than 2,000 classic films over the last 25 years.

'When I kept collecting them after they became obsolete, people said I would never get anything for them, but who's laughing now?' pointed out the 44-year-old son of two, who when asked couldn't put a figure on how much money he actually spent on the discs over the years.

'It doesn't matter how much I spent on them, what's important here is that I got money back on them when people said I was wasting my time. I proved them all wrong,' Fielding persisted, looking a bit uncomfortable at the question as this reporter calculated how much he spent.

'Yeah, but that's 20 grand old money,' he defended, when confronted with the full sum of money he had spent on the collection that he has now sold for the equivalent of the very first DVD boxset he bought, *21 Jump Street*.

'The point is I'm €75 richer than I was this morning and never listen to complete idiots who haven't a clue about anything and think they know it all when they don't, alright?' he concluded.

116

Lifestyle

## FAMILIES

# HUSBAND ONLY STAYING IN MARRIAGE FOR THE SUNDAY ROASTS

### Mindlessness Tip
Always remember that no matter how bad life can get, you can always rely on that one friend to be fucking up their life just that little bit more than you.

HUSBAND Ger Reilly would have left his wife years ago if it wasn't for her delicious Sunday roasts, *WWN* reports.

Despite having two children together, Eileen Reilly's ability to perfectly roast chicken, potato, veg and making a God-like gravy was the main reason Ger claimed they were still married after nine long years.

'The second she stops being able to make these I'm gone – 'til no Sunday roast do us part,' thought Ger, tucking into his ninth goose-fat-laced roast potato of the sitting. 'By the time Saturday hits I'm already done with her in my head but then I manage to get out for a few beers with the lads before she coaxes me back while I'm hungover the following day – the crafty bitch reels me back in for another week of it.'

Openly weeping at the dinner table, the 39-year-old swore by her stuffing as he went back for seconds before letting his wife know how much he appreciated her cooking.

'You know I love you … on Sundays,' the old romantic exclaimed, saying the last two words under his breath.

Unaware of the thin thread holding their marriage together, Eileen thanked her husband for his kind words before lovingly grabbing his hand, closing her eyes, and fantasising it was his older, wealthier, fitter-looking brother.

### Famous Quotes from 2024
"I don't think it's on social media platforms to stop the spread of misinformation. Additionally the only way I can get an erection is by rubbing my nipples while looking at a picture of Donald Trump fellating a banana"
- Elon Musk, on calls to curb the spread of misinformation on X

> 'The second she stops being able to make these I'm gone – 'til no Sunday roast do us part'

117

# Waterford Whispers News

## DRINKING

# CAMDEN STREET NAMED BEST PLACE TO HAVE DRUNKEN PUBLIC ROW WITH FRIENDS AT 2 A.M.

DUBLIN's CAMDEN Street is celebrating topping a prized list for the fifth year running after being awarded the title of 'best place to have drunken public row with friends at 2 a.m.'.

'It's the abundance of connecting side streets that do it for me, one second you're chatting to your friend, next minute she's disappeared down a lane to vomit and you're 30 minutes screaming on the phone to each other, insisting neither of you have moved an inch,' shared one frequent partaker in Camden chaos.

The fact that drunk people consistently conflate Camden Street, Wexford Street and Aungier Street, melting them into one single indecipherable street, lends itself to maximising confusion and anger among friends when agreeing to meet on Camden Street when they are in fact halfway up George's Street.

'Sitting drunk in Eddie's, aggressively insisting you are in Wow Burger to your friends on Snapchat, tell me another street that offers that, I'll wait,' said another person who has seen 17 friendships end on Camden Street this year alone.

'Due to its close proximity to Harcourt Street, it's the perfect location for one belligerent and drunk friend to stubbornly insist Camden Street is in fact Harcourt Street and that "oh my God SHUT UP, Coppers is just up here, c'mon",' confirmed one of the judging panel for this year's award.

For ageing out-of-touch revellers, recent years have seen a number of drinking spots change their names, which is a perfect ingredient in the cocktail of contentious conversations.

'Everyone's young and I'm scared, where's The Palace? Where's The Village? What have they done with it? Don't make me go to Flannery's. Why did you make me come here?' added one sobbing 40-year-old to a friend as he struggled to hear himself over the sound of students successfully flagging down a taxi he had ordered on Free Now.

### Community Alert

Anyone have a number for a frumpy babysitter with a face on her like a bulldog chewing a wasp? Taking no chances after Heaney's harlot of a daughter tempted my Sean. Contact Triona on 08666680600.

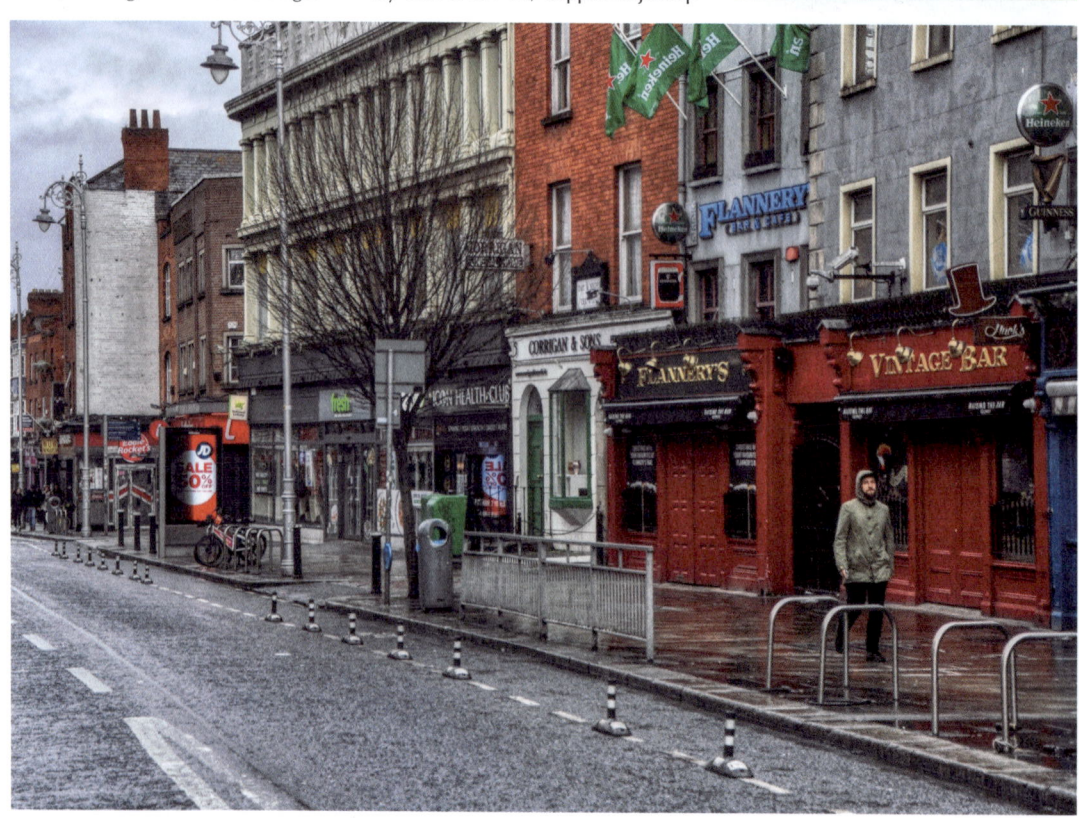

Lifestyle

## HEN PARTIES

# IRISH HEN PARTIES RISE THREE PLACES ON INTERNATIONAL LIST OF TERROR ORGANISATIONS

THERE HAVE been muted, even disappointed reactions within Irish hen circles after a joint FBI and Interpol terror watch list only ranked Irish bridal parties on the rip as the ninth most deadly terrorist fighting force in the world.

'Look it's not the result we were hoping for, we're disappointed. We get that the judges don't traditionally count hen parties so even to get into the top 10 we're punching above our weight I suppose, just like Siobhan did in Salou when she floored that fat English cow in that restaurant haha,' shared Irish woman Shannon Lonegan, a veteran of 17 hens.

For a number of years, causing havoc abroad was considered just a 'male pursuit' with Irish stags across European cities and Las Vegas causing PTSD in all those unfortunate enough to encounter them. However, in recent years Irish hen parties have ventured further and further afield, causing the blood to run cold in anyone working in the service industries.

'They always bill their piss-ups as "super chill and relaxing" but no matter what way they dress it up, no matter the spa location or yoga retreat, they inevitably get more fucked up than Conor McGregor at a christening,' confirmed one Portuguese vineyard employee, who lost an eye after telling a hen party they don't do free refills, nor do they stock '10-litre bottles of mega-wine'.

For some, making the terror list is the start of something special.

'For too long Irish women were told recording yourself getting a lap dance in Amsterdam and accidentally sending it to your partner was just for men, but I hope we've done our part in showing young girls that you too can end up on the front of the *Sunday World* in a headline like "Hacketstown Hen Arrested For Biting Dutch Policeman's Ear Off",' shared one Carlow bridesmaid.

> 'They inevitably get more fucked up than Conor McGregor at a christening'

### Did You Know?
The most common cause of divorce in Ireland is listed as 'putting their cold feet on me in bed'.

Waterford Whispers News

## CHRISTMAS

# MAKING SURE YOUR CHILD'S LETTER TO SANTA IS GDPR COMPLIANT

COMPLYING with GDPR guidelines is not something a young child writing to Santa Claus should be worrying about, which is why *WWN* has put together this handy guide for European parents to help avoid the €50k fine involved in failing to adhere to EU privacy regulations.

Due to being situated outside the EU, the North Pole has to check each individual letter to Santa to make sure it is adhering to information guidelines, which keep your children's personal information safe and private. If anything the mass kidnapping of 447,567 children from EU homes told us in 2004, it's that Santa lists can be lethal if they fall into the wrong hands.

**Never Write Surname or Address**
Every eejit knows Santa already knows where each child lives just by their first name alone. After all, Santa knows when you are sleeping, he knows when you're awake, he knows when you've been bad or good, however, as bloody Xmas day 2004 reminds us, he doesn't know when he's employing an elvish Satan-worshiping paedophile ring for over 70 years.

**Leave no Clues**
Not to keep bringing it up, but no one wants almost half a million children disappearing over the space of a year – this is not America – whatever you do make sure there are no clues in your child's wish list. No references to schools, pets, mammy and daddy, nothing; just first name, what toys they want. Remember to wipe all fingerprints and traces of DNA before sending.

**Only Send through Designated Santa Post Boxes**
Nationalised postal services will stamp locations on letters so never ever use them for Santa lists – over 25% of the slaughtered innocents of '04 used their state-run postal service. We advise leaving the letter up the chimney as a good old-fashioned organic way to send your Santa list. Certified Santa Mail centres are also a secure way, but as some survivors explained, always be accompanied by a parent when delivering the letter.

**Just Enjoy the Magical Moment**
We understand it's very hard to compartmentalise those horrific images and graphically detailed videos from Elfpocalypse 2004, but for the children's sake, just have fun with it, guys, and avoid passing on any anxieties to your children this Christmas as it could be their last.

In tomorrow's Christmas Guide edition, legally making sure Santa accepts cookies before actually eating cookies.

Lifestyle

## DINING

# BREAKING: FOOD ORDER SERVED SUSPICIOUSLY FAST

SERVED piping hot with all the signs of being nuked in a microwave, a spaghetti bolognese main ordered by local man Ger Watts came out suspiciously fast for his liking, *WWN* reports.

'I literally ordered this three minutes ago and the steam off it could run a sauna,' Watts pointed out to this reporter and not the waiting staff serving him the meal.

Not usually one to complain about quick and efficient service, Watts spent the entire sitting wondering if the dish was something they had already prepared in one of those 'keep hot things', or was it fucked into a microwave for three minutes and slapped out in front of him, Soviet kitchen style.

'It's lovely. It tastes great. A bit too hot, so there's definitely something going on here I'm not aware of. I will have to dock a few marks off it for that reason alone,' he added, now blowing on his fork to cool it down.

Preferring a slightly later delivery time, the Dublin man explained none of this suspicion would have grown in his mind if the meal took 7–10 minutes to be served.

'I wouldn't have asked any questions then,' he reveals, now picking up the bowl-like plate and inhaling the remaining minced beef and tomato sauce contents like a caveman, 'to be honest it's kind of put me off coming here again – shame, the food is gorgeous.'

# A FIRST: MAN GIVES BLOOD WITHOUT TELLING EVERYONE

RESEARCHERS investigating claims that Irish man Harry Ronan has the ability to donate blood without telling everybody about it have said they are dumbfounded, calling for further funding to help discover his secret.

The 52-year-old Kilkenny man reportedly gives blood on a regular basis, yet somehow doesn't gloat about it online or constantly bring it up with friends or family.

'He just comes in, gives his pint and leaves without so much as a word,' nurses working at a local donation centre explained. 'It's like he's doing this as a selfless act and is not looking for kind of praise or reward from his fellow peers.'

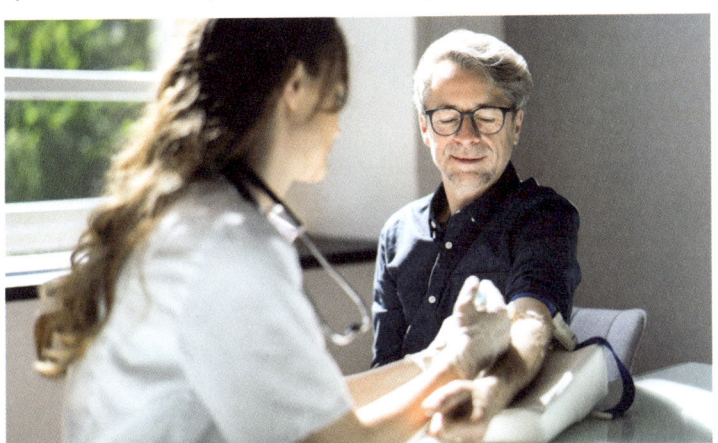

The strange phenomenon was reported late last year when Mickey Hennessy, a friend of the son of two, discovered a plaster patch on Ronan's arm, before pressing him on why it was there.

'I nearly had to beat it out of him,' Hennessy recalls. 'He first said it was "nothing", and then when I kept asking him for the following hour or two he finally caved in and revealed he gave blood – I felt it was only right to tell everyone for him. You can't just give blood like that and not boast about it.'

The news comes after the Irish Blood Transfusion Service made renewed calls for blood following depletion of stocks; it aims to always have seven days of stock on hand but in some areas, they're now down to two days. Appointments can be made by calling freephone 1800 222 111.

121

Waterford Whispers News

## MOTORING
# NOT TO BE OUTDONE, LOCAL MOTHER ARRIVES FOR SCHOOL RUN IN MONSTER TRUCK

THE SCHOOL run can often be the scene of amateur fashion shows, displays of opulence and an overall parade of pettiness as parents exhibit the sort of puerile childishness that would make their own children blush.

However, that was not the case today as mother-of-three Alex Sullivan arrived in a monster truck to drop off her children.

'I got a good trade-in on the Land Rover and the seat is just the perfect height for seeing all of the road,' confirmed Sullivan as she threw out a ladder for her children to aid their descent out of the car.

'You know, what with all the big jeeps and that, it just feels safer for me. A bit of peace of mind with the kids 'cos let's face it, there are some lunatics around here that can't drive,' added Sullivan, reversing out of a disabled parking space and over several cars she had crushed.

The inevitable evolution of school run vehicles could yet spark a purchasing frenzy.

'What I look for in a car is simple; something brand new that loses its value instantly, puts me in severe debt and above all else is beyond my capabilities to control as a driver,' explained fellow mum Grace Hartigan, who after seeing Sullivan's new purchase has vowed to buy that British army issue Challenger 3 tank she has had her eye on.

The mothers were keen to stress that before curtain twitchers in the locality have their say, they need the large vehicles on account of the fact they are always hitting the tough terrain of Ireland's countryside at least once a decade.

### Classifieds

**WHERE'S ALL THE FINTANS GONE?**

Haven't met or even heard the name Fintan in decades. Surely there must be one or two Fintans left in the country. Would love to know what happened to the name. I can understand names like Adolf, but as far as I'm aware there has been no real bad person named Fintan in the past 100 years unless I'm missing something?

If you're a Fintan please email me: Fintan_1954@hotmail.co.uk

Lifestyle

## COST OF LIVING

# FREE MEALS, ELECTRICITY, BED, GYM, ROOF OVER HEADS; PRISON NOT SOUNDING BAD NOW TO LOCAL FAMILY

'OKAY, Mark, if you go down to Londis with this toy gun and rob the place with your sister, me and your mam will continue to not pay the TV licence,' Jimmy Riordan ordered his teenage son and daughter. 'We should get a good few months out of it.'

The Riordan family are just one of hundreds of Irish families now resorting to life on the inside in a bid to avoid the spiralling cost of living on the outside.

'The O'Briens down the road murdered the Tierneys and got life, the lucky bastards,' Jimmy stated as he packed the family's belongings into boxes to put in storage while they go to prison. 'Free meals, no electricity bills, there's a bed, gym, roof over our heads and it will toughen up the kids no end; what's not to like?'

Crimes related to cost-of-living pressures have surged over the past two years with more and more people opting for a life behind bars in Ireland's cushy prisons.

'There's even a games room and library, there's more amenities here for young people than on the outside,' 17-year-old Seamus Fielding told WWN, who purposely skinned up a joint in front of a rural garda, securing himself six months rent-free inside. 'I had one friend make the mistake of paying some woman to say he assaulted her, but sure didn't the judge let him off – you gotta know the system.'

### The Year in Numbers
### 304,087
The number of Irish men who, at any given time, believe they could launch a craft beer brewery.

With prisons already maxed out, many desperate people are now resorting to other means to secure a better way of life.

'I travelled to Ukraine and then pretended I was a refugee so I could come back to Ireland and get free stuff,' David Humphries, now known as Pavel Vavreck, told WWN. 'Now I'm freezing me bollocks off in a leaky tent in a field in Laois and being called a paedo by an angry mob, but at least I get free tinned soup!'

### County Council Notices
An understandable clerical error has resulted in funding meant for the repair work on the swimming pool roof was used to build an extension to the council's chief architect's home. A mistake that could have happened to anyone.

## HOLIDAYS

# COUPLE SAVING FOR WEEKEND AWAY IN IRELAND SETTLE FOR TWO MONTHS IN BAHAMAS INSTEAD

A HARD-WORKING couple planning a night or two off from the kids in one of Ireland's sought-after holiday towns have ditched their plans in favour of two long months in the Caribbean for roughly the same price.

'When you factor in petrol, the hotel room or an Airbnb, plus there's the food you'd be eating, the price of a pint, all in all we were looking at prices in the region of "fuck off away with yourself ye thieving bastards",' confirmed local man Colm Cassidy.

'We didn't think the Bahamas would be on the radar really but it's about €8,000 each for the two months, so we're actually still coming out with savings when compared to competing with Yanks for a hotel room in Dublin or Galway,' added Colm's wife Yvonne.

A spokesperson for Fáilte Ireland pointed out that such locations could be prone to tropical storms and even hurricanes during off-peak times, which still sounded more preferable to the Cassidys than eating a breakfast an Irish hotel billed as 'the full Irish' but only contained one sausage.

'Look it, we're not saying the Bahamas suits everyone, some

> 'Some people hear about the clear water, the white sands, the heat and they'd take being rained on in Kerry for the same price'

people hear about the clear water, the white sands, the heat and they'd take being rained on in Kerry for the same price,' conceded the Cassidys.

### Mindlessness Tip
A great way to improve a relationship is by focusing on someone and really staring at them until they look away before grabbing them by the head, forcing their eyes open with your thumbs and shouting 'look at me' over and over again until they beg you to stop.

### Did You Know?
True crime podcast addiction is now an officially recognised mental disorder.

Lifestyle

## SOCIAL MEDIA
# TOUCHING! DAD REPLIES TO DAUGHTER'S LENGTHY HEARTFELT MESSAGE WITH THUMBS UP EMOJI

NOT one to hold back on his emotions, Waterford dad Tim Mackey was today praised for his heartfelt response to a beautifully worded text message from his daughter in Australia last night, WWN has learned.

Having not seen or interacted with his eldest child in over a month, Mackey brought 27-year-old Tabatha to tears with just one simple but highly effective emoji.

'When I saw dad's thumbs up response to my 1,000-word message I knew this was a father–daughter moment to cherish for the ages,' said the teary-eyed daughter of two.

Framing the interaction before hanging it on her wall as a reminder of just how strong a bond she has with her father, Tabatha revealed that the unconditional love between the two, despite them being on opposite sides of the world, is the only thing keeping her going.

'I don't know where I'd be without his support,' she went on, now staring forlornly at the single thumbs-up emoji her thoughtful middle-aged dad spent milliseconds sending. 'It's so simple, yet means so much to me. I love you too, Dad.'

Unaware of the feeling he caused, Mackey insisted it was no effort at all and that he basically uses a thumbs up emoji quite regularly and really didn't think much of it at the time.

'I liked it,' he confirmed, before giving this reporter a thumbs up.

### County Council Notices
For those unable to attend tonight's council meeting, it is available to view as an oil painting in council offices all week.

# GIRLFRIEND IN ONE OF THOSE WEIRD MOODS WHERE SHE'S HOLDING FACT YOU'RE MARRIED WITH THREE KIDS AGAINST YOU

LOCAL Nevin McDaid is at his wits' end as his girlfriend of two years Clare Clossey is in one of her weird moods again and he just can't win no matter how he tries to reason with her, WWN can reveal.

'Ah, it's her monthly or something because I came in at 2 a.m. there Tuesday night and she flipped the lid, it's like she doesn't appreciate how hard it is for me to sneak out of the house without the wife knowing,' McDaid told WWN.

'And yeah, I did say I'd leave the wife and kids but that's something you say when the young one you're riding is threatening to end things. If I'd known she thought I was serious … I'd still say it but be more vague and not agree to a timeline for leaving my family,' added McDaid, who's no sexist but some women, huh?

Arms crossed and a frown on her like a shark dipped in chilli, Ms Clossey (25) has remained non-verbal for much of the evening and is on the opposite couch to McDaid, who feels he might as well be talking to Myra Hindley, such are the evil eyes she's giving him.

'I don't know where she gets out being so mad, she knew what she was getting into when I eventually came clean a year in about having a wife and kids,' offered McDaid. 'My big fear is I've been sitting here for two hours in silence and not so much as a rope pull, and I know she's just going to flip the lid when I tell her I've to get home to the missus in a bit on account of it being our anniversary and that,' McDaid added, a man with the patience of a saint.

125

Waterford Whispers News

## RELATIONSHIPS

# MARRIED FRIENDS WONDERING WHEN ARE YOU TWO GETTING MARRIED, BUYING HOUSE, BECOMING MISERABLE LIKE THEM

DESPERATE for someone to share their existence with, married couple Tim and Lucy Williams are wondering when are you two going to succumb to the traditional lifestyle and finally become miserable like they are.

'You guys must be together forever at this stage,' Lucy quizzed while out on her one designated night of the year, hoping deep down you've agreed on a wedding date so she can stop seeing all your fantastic social media posts of you having fun together.

### The Year in Numbers

**301** The number of Irish couples who ended up in A&E after thinking a ride in the shower was a good idea.

'You've no mortgage, no kids; you guys are really missing out!' she added with a straight face.

Locked into a 35-year mortgage with their third child under five on the way, the Williams insisted having children is the best feeling in the world, pointing out time is short, and you guys aren't getting any younger.

'All those fancy sun holidays you two go on every three months are great and all, but it will never beat the feeling of owning your own home,' Tim pointed out, as news of an eleventh mortgage interest rate hike rang from the paw-printed television. 'What you need is the security of having to stay with the same partner in the same house for the next three decades, not this exciting willy-nilly day-to-day going out for meals and

### 2025 Predictions

An increase in incidents of racism in 2025 will be greeted with an increase in the number of people insisting Ireland has zero racism, so shut up.

enjoying each other's company without being bogged down with huge responsibilities kind of thing – it's unhealthy at your age.'

Excusing the row you overheard in the kitchen earlier, Tim and Lucy playfully jested they want to see an engagement ring next time you two come round, before informing you there's an affordable three-bed semi down the road for just €550k; they'll send a link to you later.

126

# WW news

Waterford Whispers News

# SPORT

Waterford Whispers News

## FOOTBALL

# TODDLER AVERTS FATHER'S TANTRUM BY PUTTING FOOTBALL ON TV

ACTING ON subtle signs little Matthew McEgan has studied and absorbed in his two years as a full-time son of two, the Waterford-based child has cut his father's latest tantrum short, masterfully managing 36-year-old Ciaran's mood swings.

'Dada look, Dada look,' implored Matthew as he mashed his banana covered fingers into the Sky remote resulting in the displaying of *Super Sunday* featuring Man United vs Spurs.

Matthew had sensed Ciaran's growing crankiness at being subjected to 40 minutes of pressing buttons on torturously loud Logitech toys and reading the same Peppa Pig story for the twelfth time in a row. These circumstances, combined with Ciaran failing to get his usual midday nap in, led Matthew to placate his father with one of his favourite distractions.

'Dada love miserable looking bollocks,' chirped Matthew as his father became transfixed by the presence of a moaning Roy Keane on the screen, Ciaran's gruff and surly demeanour long forgotten now that the 36-year-old had bright

> 'I know it's lazy of me but it keeps him happy even if it's not exactly stimulating his mind'

and colourful figures dancing across a screen.

'He lives on that thing, obsessed so he is,' confirmed Matthew to *WWN*.

'I know it's lazy of me but it keeps him happy even if it's not exactly stimulating his mind,' added Matthew before being drowned out by shouts from his father of 'more more more' as Man Utd delivered another lacklustre performance.

### Did You Know?

Prejudice is a visceral response driven by the brain's amygdala, frontal cortex, insula, striatum and medial prefrontal cortex, which is what you should say when caught out being incredibly racist.

### Mindlessness Tip

Walking is one of the most perfect opportunities to be mindful. Try walking with intention. If you are carefully focused you will begin to feel that quiet sense of peace. Apologies, I meant wank – wanking.

## Sport

### OLYMPICS

# OPENING CEREMONY CHAOS AS RUDE PARISIANS REFUSE TO HELP ATHLETES WITH DIRECTIONS

THE AWE-INSPIRING sight of an Olympic ceremony unfolding along Paris's River Seine is looking like a remote possibility as the athletes from a number of participating nations struggle to arrive at the the procession's starting point on time, hampered by the reluctance of locals to be of any help.

'Where iz zee parade yoke, on zee river, yeah?' a harried Kellie Harrington begged dozens of indifferent Parisians who steadfastly ignored the Irish Olympian despite perfectly understanding her question and knowing the exact location she was searching for.

A unique approach to the opening ceremony of the Games, having floats along the Seine, has complicated things for athletes who would have no problem getting to a stadium but now don't want to risk roaming data charges on their phones by using Google Maps.

'Je ne comprends pas,' offered the most polite Parisian encountered so far, who issued the phrase while angrily waving a stick at lost athletes.

On the lookout for people in spandex waving flags, a number of athletes accidentally joined a Pride parade in the city, while a number of gymnasts late to the ceremony found themselves at Moulin Rouge after following flexible people dressed in tight clothing.

Going against the stereotype, one kindly Parisian directed the British team directly over a bridge and into the river.

> **County Council Notices**
> A bridge lift and tuck will take place at 9 p.m. tonight due to its ageing facade.

---

# MAN PICKED LAST FOR 5-A-SIDE HAS TROUBLING FLASHBACK TO JUNIOR INFANTS PLAYGROUND

A WATERFORD man is considering whether he needs to avail of counselling after experiencing a particularly traumatic incident that preceded his weekly 5-a-side match, *WWN* understands.

'Everything sort of went silent and I could just see Simon's lips move in slow motion, and my name just never left his lips,' 5-a-side player Andrew O'Byrne recalled of the harrowing moment the usual dividing of teams left him discarded onto Tony's team after friend Simon Kelly declined to pick him.

The resulting flashbacks to an incident in junior infants when O'Byrne was excluded from a game of chasing left O'Byrne crippled by insecurity and self-doubt, leaving him unable to play to his usual fairly shite standard of 5-a-side.

'Sure I've lost a yard of pace and the ball bounces off me like I'm made entirely of landmines but fuck me, it's harsh, Simon and me have been mates for years and now Jose from his work turns up and it's like I don't exist,' said O'Byrne of Jose Caicedo, a Venezuelan national who plays like the lovechild of Ronaldinho and Messi.

O'Byrne is believed to be one of just 500,000 Irish adults who can be momentarily plunged back into their vulnerable infantile selves whenever they feel themselves being cast aside in social and sporting settings.

'And then Tony is shouting at me for missing a tackle, yeah okay Tony, but I'm actually battling with some deep-seated childhood trauma here and I didn't even want to be on your team, I wanted to be on Simon's,' O'Byrne found himself shouting while sat in the centre circle having a mini breakdown.

Waterford Whispers News

## GAA

# GAA RAFFLE WITH TOP PRIZE OF ELECTRICIAN'S PHONE NUMBER SELLS OUT IN SECONDS

SHIFTING THEIR focus from raffling off brand new houses, a number of GAA clubs are reporting record ticket sales and revenue after offering a grand prize of a phone number belonging to an electrician who is available to carry out work on homes.

'The raffle tombola has been under 24-hour armed guard since one couple in need of rewiring their house actually tried to climb into it – it's madness,' confirmed facilitator of one such draw in Waterford, Cormac Carney.

The electrician in question, Fergus Hefferty, is so coveted as a top raffle draw prize because when he tells a client he needs to head to Chadwicks for something he doesn't disappear, never to be heard from again.

With over 50,000 tickets selling out in the first week they went on sale, there have been fears the draw could be open to corruption, with bribes being offered to members of the board of St Fintan's GAA Club.

'People need to feel like this is a trustworthy draw and the reputation of the club itself would be in tatters if it wasn't all above board and there were bribes taken,' confirmed a St Fintan's member, speaking to *WWN* out the window of his brand new 2024 Mercedes S-class.

Not everyone is happy with the draw, however, with some pointing to inferior runner-up prizes.

'Second prize is €50,000! What am I going to do with that? I need a fucking spark to turn up and tell me why my living room light switches on the dishwasher,' offered one disgruntled raffle entrant.

# DIEHARD MAN UNITED FAN DISCOVERS INTENSE DISTASTE FOR ALL THINGS ENGLISH JUST IN TIME FOR THE EUROS

A LOCAL MAN who spent much of the previous nine months slavishly devoted to all things red and Manchester-based has discovered that he actually intensely dislikes all things English, *WWN* Sport has learned.

'They'd sicken your hole,' confirmed Tony Nealon, who treats the ups and downs of the goings-on at a Manchester club as if it were life and death.

'Even a glimpse of that red and white flag is enough to make you vomit, the way they go on, you'd love to see them crash out,' insisted Nealon, who had no idea he hated the likes of Harry Maguire, Luke Shaw and Kobbie Mainoo so much.

Nealon is believed to be one of a possible total of five or six Irish people who have fervent devotion and encyclopedic knowledge of a club located in a country they would happily see burned to the ground during the duration of Euro 2024 and other major tournaments.

'Big English head on him, that's a fivehead, not a forehead, and he's a gurrier too, was arrested in Greece but the commentators won't mention that though. Wouldn't get that in the GAA,' he continued of an English man who he regularly references when using the phrases 'we played well' and 'our pressing is shite'.

'It's the way they go on, the music, the clothes, their crap food. Everything, there's not one redeeming feature, how anyone could be rooting for them is beyond me,' added Nealon while nearly bankrupting himself by booking tickets for a Man United pre-season friendly set to take place in a few weeks.

## FOOTBALL

# EURO 2024 GIVES BOYFRIEND RARE CHANCE TO WATCH FOOTBALL EVERY NIGHT

A WOMAN concerned for her football-loving boyfriend is said to be relieved at news of a tournament called 'the Euros', which is broadcasting three games a day for the next month, *WWN* has learned.

'He never gets the chance to sit down and give out to millionaires kicking a ball on TV, it's such a rare thing that when I heard the Euros was on I nearly cried for him,' shared local woman Jess Daly, as her boyfriend Kevin Cooley settled in for Germany vs Scotland, the first of 51 matches over the coming weeks.

'It always shocks me how little of it is on TV, there would be long passages of time, we're talking minutes, when Kevin goes without live football on the TV but thankfully the Euros has come along to fix that,' explained Daly, who is sad that Cooley will have to miss his godson's birthday but understandably Slovenia vs Denmark must take priority.

Cooley for his part is keenly aware that such a large volume of football could overstimulate his mind, and has taken steps to offset any negatives effects.

'Usually during the season you'd only get live football on Saturday, Sunday, Monday, Tuesday, Wednesday and Thursday but with the Euros there's also games on Friday, I've had to quadruple the beer stored in the fridge and there's 10 extra bags of Doritos,' explained Cooley, who has also taken the step to attach the TV screen directly onto his retina so no outside influences disrupt his football time.

'It's great he has this, sometimes I worry he spends too much time with me, y'know,' concluded Daly, who looks forward to next conversing with her boyfriend five weeks and one Euros final from now.

### Community Alert

Hi everyone, would really appreciate people buying raffle tickets for GAA club, we're arranging it so we win the car prize but will make sure one of you win the €500 prize.

131

Waterford Whispers News

## MMA

# McGREGOR NEARING FINAL SCENE IN SCARFACE PHASE

AS PARANOIA sets in following years of overindulgence and quickly falling down the rabbit hole, former sports icon and now full-time hate monger Conor McGregor is believed to be at the 'final scene of Scarface' phase of his life, experts have confirmed.

Realising his fanbase can be broadened and collective IQ reduced by spouting outrage about migrants online, McGregor stared at his X feed like it was Tony Montana's security cameras as torrents of critics closed in and flooded his phone screen.

'You wanna play rough, okay, this is war,' the once admired fighter exclaimed, unaware of how similar his own life is to the 1983 classic where a man from a disadvantaged background goes from rags to riches in the land of the free. 'The world is mine and everything in it,' he added incorrectly, presuming money equals respect as fan-boy yes-men egged him closer to his inevitable final chapter.

'Say hello to my little politically motivated friend,' the now worse-for-wear looking 35-year-old shouted, brandishing a list of far-right dog whistles, well known to be the last port of call for once successful people when all respect has evaporated. 'Ireland for the Irish!' he roared from the comfort of his multi-million-dollar Las Vegas home, an income-tax-free state far from the one he left behind, but continues to rile.

'You'll do nothin',' a defiant McGregor said, as reality encircled him ahead of his demise.

## FOOTBALL

# CALLING AN U-8S REFEREE A CUNT AND OTHER SIGNS YOU'RE SETTING A GOOD EXAMPLE FOR YOUR CHILD

IT CAN BE hard to strike the balance of supportive parent and a referee-abusing nutjob when on the sideline of your child's U-8s match.

You want to believe you're setting the right example, and yet many a parent has been left guilt-ridden by the realisation that while they gently encouraged their child to realise 'it's all a bit of fun' they forgot to call the referee a cunt.

If you're left with the same horrible feeling every weekend that you're not being the best role model, here are some telltale signs that you're only getting in your head about it all and that you are in fact knocking it out of the park.

You're a multi-tasker; not only are you teaching your child the rules of the road and how to maintain your car without being pulled over by the police, you're also smashing in the brake light on the referee's car.

You utter the phrase, 'no son, if the first punch breaks the nose you can just leave it at that. They've probably learned their lesson.'

Thanks to your immensely helpful headbutt of another father on the sideline, you've shown your child how to 'de-escalate the situation'.

Your child is developing that 'never give up' attitude thanks to your dedication to still threatening the life of the referee long after he's called off the game.

You spend the following evening saying 'they've taken it completely out of context' when the *Six One News* only shows a brief snippet of the viral video from the match, which unfairly shows you on the sideline, slide tackling a grandmother in a motorised wheelchair.

## Sport

### GAA

# SURGERY TO FREE MAN FROM HIS GAA TRAINING TOP UNSUCCESSFUL

DESPITE the best efforts of a leading medical team at St Vincent's Hospital in Dublin, a 39-hour surgery has ended in failure as a Meath man remains trapped in his GAA training top.

'You think I wear this every day by choice? What lunatic wears the one GAA top into work, training, dinner with the missus, the school run, funerals, weddings, the whole gamut of social occasions? This is a living, waking nightmare, get it off me now,' Meath man Gerry Reardon was heard saying to family members in the run-up to surgery, which has sadly not achieved the desired outcome.

The surgery was initially complicated by the fact the patient couldn't remove his clothing when donning a gown, and tempers flared when, despite being under heavy anesthetic, Reardon instinctively lashed out at anyone trying to take the top off his body, such was the severity of his GAA-based loyalty and pride.

'It has formed a type of symbiosis with Reardon and therefore to separate them could risk killing him, it's like were Reardon to take it off he would cease to be himself, there would be nothing left, no definition to his being,' explained exhausted surgeon Dr Ranbir Khan.

The last known photo of Reardon without his local club's GAA training top on dates back to his baptism, with people unsure if the top grew in size with the 32-year-old as he aged or if it shed like snakeskin only to emerge in a renewed and stronger coating.

'I just feel guilty I suppose,' shared a visibly dejected Reardon. 'I have this sneaking suspicion I'm contagious; all the lads on the team, the coaches, my sons, they've got this bastard affliction too and maybe I gave it to them,' added Reardon, now donning a second GAA top in the hope of tricking the first top into loosening its grip on him.

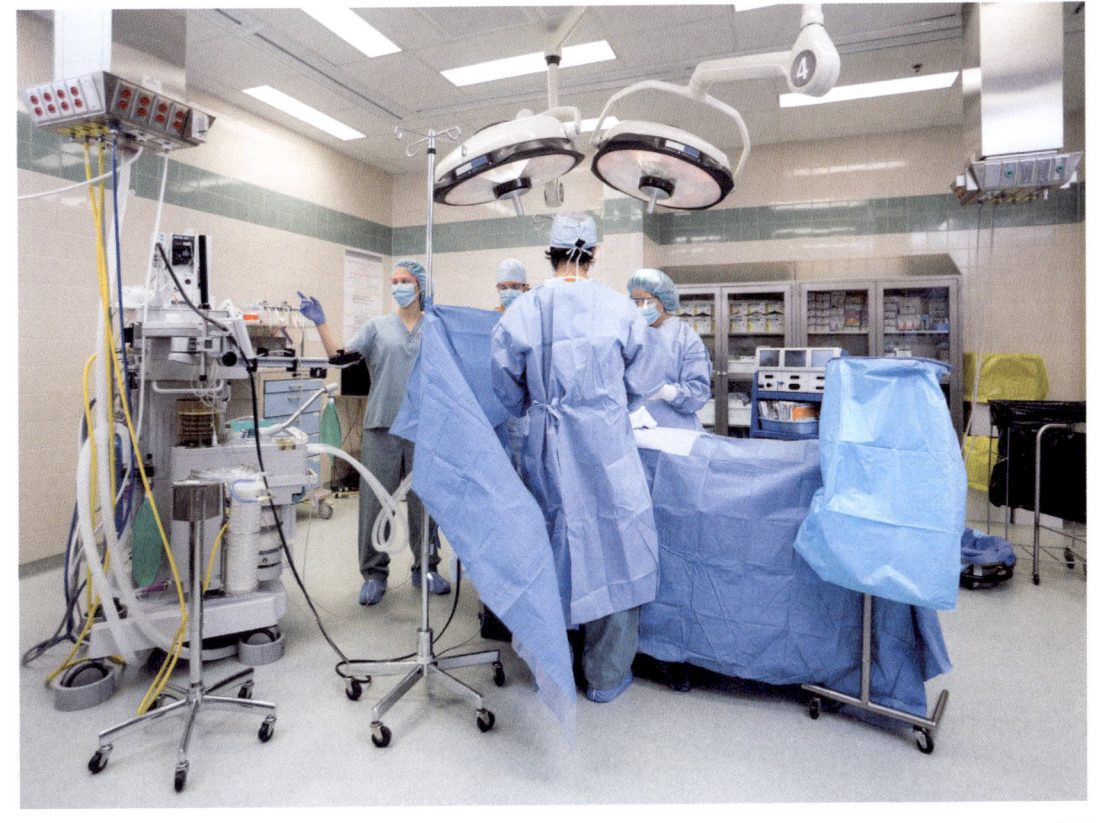

Waterford Whispers News

## ROAD BOWLING

# ROAD BOWLER TESTS POSITIVE FOR PERFORMANCE-ENHANCING DRUGS

SENDING shockwaves throughout the world of Irish road bowling, local star Mossey 'The Slingshot' Flemming was not available for comment today after testing positive for anabolic steroids, *WWN* has learned.

Doping control officers confirmed that local Woodstown champion Flemming had been using controlled substances after several complaints from fellow competitors alleged he 'must be on something with the throw on him'.

'Knew it,' Kilkenny road bowling champion Micky Ryan told *WWN* today. 'Sure he had a fucking arm on him like Popeye the last year – we slagged him off saying he must be constantly wanking the lad off himself, but it all makes sense now, the cheating bastard.'

Destroying all his competition last year, Flemming quickly rose to fame, attracting model girlfriends including Una Healy and Linda Martin, and more recently turning up to a rural road event in Fenor in a Bugatti Veyron, presumably purchased with the proceeds of his unfair winnings.

'Heard most of his post-bowling after-parties ended up as drug-fuelled orgies in local community centres and would last days on end,' one source stated, pointing out that CSO statistics have also shown a 60% rise in the number of women aged 50+ becoming pregnant. 'He's rumoured to have at least one child in every county – that's all the testosterone now, the randy hoor.'

Flemming is expected to be stripped of all his road bowling titles this year and banned from the sport for at least a week and a half.

> **'He's rumoured to have at least one child in every county – that's all the testosterone now, the randy hoor.'**

### County Council Notices

Cyclists in a hurry coming to a red light should mount the footpath bypassing the traffic lights before entering the road again without stopping. NOTE: Not advised for motorists.

### Did You Know?

The average Irish man's breath smells like a wet sock that got a job cleaning out the bins of a kebab shop.

## Sport

### GAA

# THE FULL TERMS OF THE 'SUPERVALU PARK' DEAL

DISCORD within the GAA community continues as debate surrounding the potential renaming of Páirc Uí Chaoimh to SuperValu Páirc rumbles on despite an announcement that plans for such a move may have been paused.

The naming rights for the stadium are believed to be valued at €250,000 a year by Cork GAA but leaked details seen by *WWN* suggest a potential sponsor gets plenty more bang for their buck than just their name hanging over the stadium with the terms including:

- Match balls and sliotars being brought to the centre of the field right before kick off in a rickety SuperValu trolley;
- Ticket checkers being replaced by self-service ticket machines;
- A beep sounding every time a player in possession crosses over the 42 line;
- All physio gear bags being replaced by SuperValu bags for life;
- Marty Morrissey commentating from behind a SuperValu checkout;
- Points scored by players being automatically added as points on their Real Rewards card;
- All food within the stadium being provided by the Happy Pear;
- Chatting pensioners blocking all exits as part of crowd control measures; and
- Discounted ticket prices for SuperValu customers who spend over €2,000 a month in stores.

UPDATE: In an attempt to quell unrest a compromise has been agreed whereby all SuperValu branches will be renamed Páirc Uí Chaoimh.

# MAN INVOLVES HR AFTER DRAWING ALBANIA IN OFFICE EURO 2024 SWEEPSTAKES

A DUBLIN office has been embroiled in a HR nightmare after an employee levelled a damaging accusation that risks ruining worker harmony and tanking the firm's reputation, *WWN* has learned.

'Fucking Albania though? And how convenient Tom's little work boyfriend Steve got France, how predictable and I'm going to say it … corrupt,' raged junior account manager Simon O'Brien, as he faced up to the prospect of wasting €50 on the office's Euro 2024 sweepstakes.

'How can I go out there and give my best for the company when I've this on my mind, I want to see serious punishment. I feckin' love the sweepstakes, this is my summer ruined,' insisted long-serving UniqueCo Office Systems employee O'Brien, distraught at having got a team that counts Chelsea's 14th choice striker as among their best players.

O'Brien immediately demanded HR manager Susan Corgan give him the Workplace Relations Commission's number if Corgan was going to insist on laughing in his face.

'This isn't a pay dispute or sexual impropriety, Susan, this is serious! Kelly got Germany and she doesn't even like football!' O'Brien said, now stamping his feet, on the verge of tears.

Tom Higgins, organiser of the office sweepstakes, denies all wrongdoing or ever having taken a bribe to assign someone to a certain team, and suggested the fact he drove into work in a 2024 BMW 8 series coupé is pure coincidence.

### The Year in Numbers

**0** The number of husbands caught staring intently at the arses of Olympic beach volleyball players on TV.

# Waterford Whispers News

## GAA

# DOZENS OF NEW COUNTIES POP UP FOLLOWING JP McMANUS GAA DONATIONS

THE GREATEST geographical upheaval Ireland has ever seen has occurred today after hitherto unheard-of counties sprouted up overnight, each one looking to avail of a €1m donation from billionaire JP McManus for their county board.

'Do we give you our bank details or how does this work?' a representative from the Eastmeath GAA county board said in an email to JP McManus.

'Ah come on, you absolutely have heard of Faffen, it has the Bunnakeady Mountains, Lough Fliuch and sure isn't Hollywood actor Cormac McCormick from here. Anyway, I've taken the liberty of filling out the cheque for you, you just need to sign it here,' shared an enthusiastic GAA official for County Faffen, which apparently borders Galway, Laois and Wexford.

The appeals made by several new counties have been rejected out of hand for their obviously made-up nature; these include Paois, Merry, Fublin, Dicklow and Cork.

Elsewhere, Irish tax experts confirmed it really is this easy to avoid scrutiny of your tax affairs as a billionaire in Ireland.

'Chuck a few quid to charity too and you'll be labelled a legend,' confirmed one accountant who specialises in putting money where Irish Revenue services can't touch it.

Meanwhile, a local man on an average salary has been told that he actually does still owe that income tax he refuses to pay despite giving a homeless person €50 last week.

# DOCTOR TELLS MAN WHO RAN DUBLIN MARATHON HIS 'NIPPLES WILL NEVER BE THE SAME'

SOME 48 hours on from the excruciating hell that is the Dublin marathon, local man Ian Reilly remains in A&E with a debilitating case of 'fried pepperoni nips' brought on by the friction between his marathon singlet and his chafed nipples.

'It's like you've been breastfeeding twins made entirely out of barbed wire, oh boy,' said a shocked Dr Farooq Ahmed, treating Reilly after a brief day's wait in A&E.

'I've seen less blood at a Halloween Horror movie marathon,' added Dr Ahmed to Reilly while beckoning in med students to observe this rare and hilarious bloodbath.

The real tragedy is that Reilly's 18 agonising hours waiting in A&E for treatment meant 18 hours of not being in a condition to upload nauseating selfies of the marathon to social media accompanied by lengthy statements about resilience filled with empty CEO podcast jargon.

While overall winner of the marathon, Ethiopian Kemal Husen, completed the course in two hours and six minutes, Reilly finished it in just 436 screams of 'me fuckin' nips'.

Reilly's suffering has done some good, however, as Ireland's current blood donation shortage has been solved by a nurse simply following the 40-year-old runner around while placing a bucket under his chest.

Sport

**MMA**

# FUTUREWATCH: CONOR McGREGOR'S FIRST 24 HOURS AS PRESIDENT

FLIRTING with the idea of running for the largely ceremonial role of president, what would an Ireland under the rule of serial court attender Conor McGregor look like?

Using state-of-the-art technology, *WWN* peers into the future to reveal the decisions President McGregor would make in his first 24 hours.

Blanchardstown District Court is moved to McGregor's back garden so his commute is reduced.

New law: to be eligible to serve in McGregor's government you must copy your new president and regularly socialise with a senior member of the Kinahan cartel in the Black Forge.

Everyone is forced to take an 'Irish patriot's exam'. You must, like McGregor, answer 'yes' to the question, 'did I triple the rents on a property I own, forcing an Irish family-run business operating for over 70 years out of business?'

All drug sniffer dogs at airports are made redundant.

All eateries in Ireland are nationalised, thus placing them under his control. They are then converted into a chain called 'Ireland Is Full' and Supreme Leader McGregor only serves patriotic Irish meals such as Guinness stew protein shakes. However, they immediately shut down when their low-paid staff from immigrant backgrounds are all deported.

To ensure the safety of Irish women, which is definitely a concern of his, a selection of the best-looking women are forced to stay with the president in Áras an Uachtaráin.

He signs a historic €2bn deal with a Dubai-based Irish manufacturing consortium to provide Áras an Uachtaráin with a month's supply of talcum powder.

An amnesty is declared for anyone who burns out the car of an individual who has accused McGregor of sexual abuse.

In a bid to undo the hellish path Ireland was on, towards a progressive and secular society, President McGregor demands Irish people once again embrace religion and God. Worries are quickly dispelled, though, as McGregor confirms it's the type of religious devotion that has loopholes; such as cheating on your missus.

Artem Lobov is banned from entering Ireland again for making McGregor admit in court he promised to pay Lobov $1m for his involvement in the Notorious whiskey brand.

A new law states that when President McGregor gets his hole licked by Elon Musk on X, it doesn't count as 'gay'.

**Community Alert**

Estate-wide ban on any residents looking for money for a charity fun run. 5k is fuck all distance and walking the thing is no achievement (yes, I'm calling you out, Aoife Carmody!)

137

Waterford Whispers News

## FOOTBALL

# LAD LOGS INTO SOCIAL MEDIA ACCOUNT HE RARELY USES TO POST RANDOM FOOTBALL STATEMENT

'NO way was that offside, VAR is a shambles,' posted rarely seen social media user Neil Tobin today, after what seems like a two-year hiatus from social media feeds.

The cryptic football post left those lucky enough to see it bewildered.

'Who the fucking hell is this aimed at?' asked one friend, who hasn't seen or heard from Tobin in a decade. 'You can't say nothing for years and then just rock up onto your social media with a vague football quote, mate, I forget who you even support.'

The bizarre update has sparked some experts in social media psychology to analyse Tobin's mindset, likening him to someone who suffers from Tourette's Syndrome.

'We believe Football TS may be an actual condition as this kind of behaviour is fairly common with "lads" in their late thirties upwards,' Professor Martin Green explained his diagnosis. 'We have found that the sufferers are usually watching a game at home on their own surrounded by their family so they've no real way to vent their opinions or converse and feel the need to instead voice them online, even if no one cares or indeed reads their posts.'

It is believed the condition also causes the sufferer to constantly check

> 'We believe Football TS may be an actual condition as this kind of behaviour is fairly common'

on how their random football posts are doing every five minutes before deleting them the following day out of the shame caused by them not receiving any interactions.

### 2025 Predictions
Ryan Reynolds is announced as the new face of Shaws department stores.

### Famous Quotes from 2024
"Look at it this way, they'll have a great paralympic team this year"
- Benjamin Netanyahu, on entering the hall of shame for war criminals

Sport

## GAA

# PEOPLE PLANNING VIOLENT ASSAULTS URGED TO TAKE UP INTER-COUNTY HURLING TO AVOID JAIL

IN THE WAKE of Limerick hurler Kyle Hayes receiving a two-year suspended sentence for his part in a violent assault, the legal community in Ireland is issuing new advice and directives for would-be violent thugs intent on assaulting people.

'Can you believe this; I had one idiot client who assaulted someone inside a venue and then again outside a venue, ran away from the guards, denied he did it forcing a trial at the taxpayer's expense – exactly like Kyle Hayes – but the eejit never took up GAA so he's serving three years. Some people intending to violently assault someone have no sense,' shared one barrister who wants people to heed his advice.

'My sincere advice to anyone out there who plans on beating someone so severely they have blurred vision, severe headaches and require surgery on their face is to get practising your sideline cuts now or else you have zero chance of a judge saying it "won't benefit society" to jail them.'

Elsewhere, GAA pundits said Limerick manager John Kiely's character statement on behalf of Kyle Hayes being instrumental in the avoidance of a jail sentence must rank as highly as any All-Ireland win in his sporting achievements.

'A case like this prompts the question, is it time the All-Stars create an award for Best Avoider of Consequences and Sure He's Just a Young Lad Letting Off Steam? Celebrating all GAA-based achievements is important,' offered one pundit.

'Anyway, violent assaults are famously victimless crimes. The real crime here? People being mean about Kyle Hayes.'

UPDATE: A local drug gang specialising in intimidation and beatings has announced a mid-term Cúl Camp for any young people looking to get into repeatedly assaulting people.

# WATERFORD MAN WINS 'WORST DRESSED' AT PUNCHESTOWN FESTIVAL

WATERFORD fashion disasteristas are hailing the efforts of one of their own today after city native Noel Slattin received the coveted title of Worst Dressed at the annual Punchestown racing festival.

Pairing stain-riddled jeans with a hoodie and a shirt so crumpled and congealed it looks like it was last ironed when the punt was still in circulation, it was Slattin's decision to pair it all with scuffed square-toed brown shoes that secured him the title with the voting judges.

'Usually we award the crown to a man who looks like his mam tried to stuff him back into his communion suit, if he bought his communion suit off a blind child working to a tight deadline in a sweatshop, but there's a certain je ne sais quoi about Noel here,' remarked one judge as he handed Slattin his novelty cheque for a chicken fillet roll with an all-you-can-eat side of coleslaw.

'It takes as much time and effort to dress this poorly as it does to dress well, people don't realise that, the ignorance is something else,' beamed Slattin, as he was raised up over his shoulders by a gaggle of bootcut-jeans-and-brown-shoe-wearing supporters.

'Years of preparation and hard work went into this. Do you know how much energy it takes over the course of a life to never retain any information in relation to sleeve length, collar size, colour clashing and all that stuff? This belly gut doesn't dangle over my belt like a frozen waterfall over a cliff by accident. Attention to detail boi, that's what it's all about!'

The moment was bittersweet for Slattin, who couldn't celebrate it alongside the man who taught him how not to dress, his father, due to the fact Slattin Sr was doing his once-in-a-decade shop for new socks and jocks.

'When Mr Slattin told me he didn't get dressed with the lights off, that impressed me, it's rare to see such an inability to pick out something half decent to wear. It's vomit for the eyeballs. Bravo,' said one judge of the contest.

Waterford Whispers News

## POOL

# LADS ROCKING IN THINKING THEY CAN JUST TAKE OVER THE POOL TABLE HAVE ANOTHER THING COMING, FINDS STUDY

A COUPLE of right boyos rocking into one local pub have another thing coming if they think they can just rack up without playing the current standing champion of the table first, a study carried out by regulars has found.

Ordering two pints of stout before casually sticking a euro into the coin slot, 'the lads' were quickly stopped in their tracks by reigning winner Jimpie Furlong, who quickly pointed to his marker on the table.

'That's a tiny piece of blue cue chalk,' the braver of the two lads interrupted, forcing Furlong's back up even more.

'That's how we do things around here; you play the winner if you want to take the table,' Jimpie barked, an air about him like he owned the pub despite being barred four times in the last year for being what onlookers described as 'a headwrecking prick'.

'Doubles – fiver a man,' Jimpie added, with fellow regulars nodding in agreement like some kind of elders deciding the fate of a villager's adulterous wife, forcing the visitors into play.

With the rack broken up by a shot that rattled the pool room, a tense game ensued as the whole pub watched on, distracted only once by a cheer generated from a smashed glass. A brief 'two shots on the black' argument was quickly resolved by a grubby handwritten 'pool rules' poster stuck to the wall with chewing gum. 'Good game,' Furlong told the losing team. 'Best of three?'

### Classifieds

**COMEDIAN WANTED FOR LOCAL RADIO SLOT**

Are you a lesser-known comedian who just never made it? Can you talk continuously about nothing for two hours without stopping for a single breath? Portlaw Local Radio is looking for a non-edgy, super-safe-content-loving early morning presenter to prop up one of our senior veteran broadcasters who'll hate every molecule of your being. Must be annoyingly chirpy and insist on doing social media videos despite working in radio.

Fax James on 051-5784562

Sport

## GYM TRAINING

# MAN UNDER FALSE IMPRESSION PEOPLE WANT TO SEE VIDEOS OF HIM WORKING OUT

### The Year in Numbers

**27** Gold medals Ireland would have won at the Olympics if we'd hired a Russian doctor.

DESPITE never receiving any indication that anyone watches his workout videos, local man Jeremy Haden continues to record himself in the gym doing gym things before then taking the time to upload them to his social media channels, *WWN* reports.

Documenting his bench presses, squats and lunges, the now fully grown adult has left scrolling family members and friends perplexed as to his reasoning for the daily dose of mundane exercise vlogging.

'No one asked for this,' long-time friend-for-now Danny Roche pointed out. 'The only thing I hate more than going to the gym is seeing videos of other people in the gym – I'd rather rub my eyes with industrial sandpaper.'

Experts believe the phenomenon of going to a public gym and positioning your phone camera in such a way that it records yourself lifting things in a repetitive motion is caused by an underlying narcissism, which is a precursor to the blossoming of a full-time career in fitness.

'They usually start like everyone going to the gym, but then when they start seeing the results they feel obliged to share their newly formed physique with everyone else,' psychologist Professor Jane Hartley explains. 'Normally if they don't get reactions to their videos they'll get bored and just stop, but if they get even a whiff of a like or a comment they'll start moving on to the next stage, personal training.'

> **'The only thing I hate more than going to the gym is seeing videos of other people in the gym'**

### 2025 Predictions

Ireland's men's football team will create at least two chances in front of goal. These two own goals will rank high among the nation's 2025 sporting achievements.

Waterford Whispers News

## RUNNING

# 'SOMEONE PLEASE HELP ME!' MAN WHO RAN LENGTH OF AFRICA UNABLE TO STOP

'JUST shoot me in the legs or something,' pleaded athlete Russ Cook today after reaching his goal of running the length of Africa.

Despite celebrations all round, the 'Hardest Geezer' urged spectators to do something to stop his legs from running another 16,000km.

**Mindlessness Tip**

Are you a minor celebrity or sports star who was sad once? Queue up at your local book publisher where they're just handing out book deals.

'It's great that I raised £600k for charity, but seriously I'd rather die than go back all this way again – I just can't stop these pair of bastards running,' Cook was heard shouting as people cheered him on. 'Seriously, someone please help me, I'm in agony here … arghhh … my fucking legs … arghhh.'

Cook, from Worthing, West Sussex, was initially joined by supporters as he crossed the finish line in Ras Angela, Tunisia, before then failing to stop and continuing on past waiting fans and family members who were there to celebrate his world record.

**Famous Quotes from 2024**

"Upon my death, whatever you do, don't blame Vlad, he's actually very nice and even more handsome than people realise"
- Alexei Navalny

'He just kept going like Forrest Gump, screaming at people to put an end to it,' one spectator recalled of the historic moment. 'He's gone now to God knows where and I guess he's going to come back around again whether he likes it or not.'

# ww news
## Waterford Whispers News

# PROPERTY

Waterford Whispers News

## SNAKES

# LOST TEXT REVEALS ST PATRICK FORGOT TO EXPEL SNAKES FROM IRISH CONSTRUCTION INDUSTRY

A NEWLY uncovered text dating back to the eighth century AD details Saint Patrick's regret for forgetting to expel all the snakes from the Irish construction industry, *WWN* reports.

The newly deciphered text written on goatskin explains that the patron saint apologised to the people of Ireland on his death bed for leaving reptiles in the sector, revealing he himself was bribed by contractors who constructed several churches for Patrick back in the day.

'It seems everyone has been vulnerable to these snakes for a long time,' historian Professor Conal Davies said. 'Patrick agreed to leave the snakes in the construction industry if they built monasteries and churches for him as part of a deal, but later said it was his biggest regret, stating that these creatures will eventually ruin the country someday – and how right he was,' Davies added. Professor Davies has been researching the parchment for the past few months.

More recently an RTÉ *Prime Time* report shed further light on our current construction industry's numerous failings and dodgy dealings, detailing how two individuals, operating as a self-styled environmental non-governmental organisation, systematically objected to planning applications to extract money from developers. 'This is the tip of the snake-berg,' one source in the industry told us today. 'The Irish construction industry makes the Italian mafia look like a Bugsy Malone nativity play.'

### Mindlessness Tip
Turns out you can buy a birthday cake any time you want as an adult, nobody checks.

> 'It seems everyone has been vulnerable to these snakes for a long time'

### County Council Notices
'Denied' stamp for planning permission requests has worn away to nothing, anyone got a spare one?

Property

## HOUSE PRICES

# HOUSE PRICES NOW HIGHER THAN YOUR UNCLE TONY AT A STAG IN AMSTERDAM

IRISH house prices are now higher than your uncle Tony walking around the red-light district in Amsterdam during a stag party after a cocktail of drugs and booze, a new CSO report has published.

Tony, notorious for his wild shenanigans, has been surprised by how high house prices have soared in Ireland, with your uncle pointing out that there is a 'huge bloody comedown' due very soon.

'I may be off my noodle, but I know one thing is for certain: what goes up, must come down,' Tony explained, puking into a canal like it was a natural thing to do before carrying on and casually wiping bits of digested burger off the picture of his friend's face printed on his stag T-shirt. 'The higher you go, the harder the landing is and just like I'm not looking forward to tomorrow, the Irish property market will be in the same condition in the next couple of years.'

Despite never owning a home, or holding down a relationship for more than three weeks, Tony warned that this 'property comedown' was going to be far worse than the one in 2008, much like his legendary hangover from your mum's wedding in 2004 where he was found sleeping naked on the hotel stairs after soiling the carpet, shutting down the hotel for three days and costing the family over two grand in cleaning fees.

'It doesn't take an expert to see where it's all going,' Tony concluded, before necking three adult portions of hallucinogenic truffles into himself like there was no tomorrow.

### Did You Know?

Children's Hospital contractors BAM began building the Sagrada Familia in 1882 with an original budget of just two pesetas.

## COUPLE GET HOUSE ON HIRE PURCHASE

A COUNTY Tipperary couple has revealed they have moved into the property of their dreams through a revolutionary new hire purchase scheme facilitated by their bank.

'All we had to do was put down a small initial down payment of €42,000 and we were allowed to move in almost immediately,' revealed Mary Brophy, who availed of the brand new scheme with her husband, Ger.

'It's a bit of a risk forking out that kind of money because if we miss a payment the house could be taken away from us but it's the only way we could secure a home for our future family,' Ger said, before outlining the process. 'The repayments also vary depending on global interest rates, which isn't great as there's no real cap on them, it's a huge financial risk we're willing to take – it's worth it to be able to pretend to our friends that we own the house.'

A hire purchase (HP) agreement is a credit agreement where you hire an item and pay an agreed amount in monthly instalments; however, you do not own the item until you have made the final payment.

'The guy in the bank called it a "death pledge" or "mortgage" and it's kind of like a fun game people play to see if they make the payments all the way to the end – it's quite exciting,' Mary recalled, before concluding, 'sure, if we don't fulfil the pledge the banks simply just take the house back, so what harm? It's all just a bit of fun.'

# Waterford Whispers News

## ON THIS DAY

# Waterford Whispers News

VOL 1, 686 — MONDAY, JUNE 7, 1952 — 1d

## Construction Begins On Cliffs Of Moher

BORD FÁILTE have announced the fledgling Irish State's most ambitious civil engineering project, eclipsing the huge scale and undertaking that was the Poulaphouca hydroelectric station in Wicklow.

The fabricated 'Cliffs of Moher' are being constructed with a working force of 1,583 men in a bid to fill the dearth of tourist attractions on the island. The hope is American tourists will make the journey to Ireland to visit the man-made marvel and purchase a great number of novelty key rings, creating thousands of punts in revenue for the beleaguered country.

Built using leftover slate from social housing construction and industrial amounts of glue, the 702ft facade will tower over the coastline and replace the eyesore of a beach currently located in Lahinch, Clare. Beginning today, 7 June 1952, the construction is expected to be complete in time for the 1960 tourist season.

'A touristic venture, aimed at beckoning exiled generations to their ancestral home, is of paramount economic importance to this island. State-of-the-art data entry shows us that Ireland has received exactly 109 tourists in the last decade, 18 of whom were here because they had gotten lost on their way to Portugal. We hope to double the number of visitors within the first decade the Cliffs are fully operational,' Fianna Fáil's Minister for External Affairs Frank Aiken confirmed to Waterford Whispers News.

The Cliffs will become just the fourth tourist attraction in Ireland, after the nation's many cows, Newgrange and a sozzled Brendan Behan.

*Continued on Page 2*

## HOUSING

### 'EACH HOUSE WILL CLAIM TO HAVE A D4 ADDRESS'; INSIDE RYANAIR'S SWORDS ACCOMMODATION

FOLLOWING Ryanair's confirmation that the company has bulk-bought 25 of 28 homes for cabin crew staff in a Swords housing estate, *WWN* looks inside O'Leary Grove to see just what it entails for employees.

- Despite being situated on the northside, each home will claim to be located in Dublin 4.
- The housing estate will have two lanes: priority and non-priority.
- Each bedroom will contain 10 beds and have a maximum closet volume of 10kg, with upgrades available at €2k per extra kilo.
- Despite rent costing just €14.99 per day, every household appliance will have a coin slot along with charges to use the one and only toilet in the entire house, which will be airplane-sized.
- Trumpets will play every time a staff member returns from work.
- When a staff member wants to move out, they will receive a smartarse reply from the Ryanair social media account every time they look for their security deposit back.
- The 25 homes will be at the furthest point away from the entrance.

146

## PLANNING

# 'AS SOMEONE ON THE PROPERTY LADDER IT'S MY DUTY TO STOP OTHERS JOINING IT,' INSISTS SERIAL OBJECTOR

'THE second I bought my home for €12,500 in 1992 I knew things had to change in the Irish property market,' writes serial planning objector Colin Woods.

The 67-year-old retiree is one of dozens of Waterford homeowners who simply hate the idea of any new developments being built in their area for no other reason than being cantankerous old bollockses with nothing better to do than stick their burst-blood-vessel noses into everyone else's business.

'An apartment block to cater for the ongoing housing crisis? Renters, no less! Not on my watch, there's no way I'm letting God knows what into my neighbourhood. We'll just claim there's not enough amenities or transport services, that usually works,' Woods said. Elaborating on his tactics, he added, 'failing that it's straight to a local councillor mate of mine to get him involved and the residents' association who are all made up of homeowners who got their homes for peanuts back in the day but somehow have the gall to still look down upon people who rent like they're the shit between their toes.'

Objecting to construction has become middle Ireland's favourite pastime at a time when over half a million Irish young people still live at home with their parents, while local councils underspend hundreds of millions of euros year-on-year without any explanation as to why they're not doing the jobs they've been paid handsomely to do.

'Yes, my home is now worth 30 times what it was when I bought it and it would take an average worker today 90 years to pay for it, but we can't have cheap apartments littering up the derelict sites in our area, these young snowflakes have it too easy,' Woods stated. 'Over my dead body,' he concluded, not realising this is what everyone is hoping for him right now.

> **Famous Quotes from 2024**
> 
> "This is the year I'm finally going to give up the drink" – Ian Bailey

Waterford Whispers News

## HOMELESSNESS

# ARMY CALLED IN AS HOMELESS MAN SPOTTED EYEING UP VACANT PROPERTY

CLONMEL town centre was closed off this morning due to a standoff between the Irish Army and a homeless man who was reportedly caught looking into the window of one of the many vacant properties in the area, *WWN* has learned.

Threatening to sleep rough in the property to escape what he claims is 'cold and wet weather', snipers took to the roofs of nearby buildings – also vacant – to make sure the man doesn't do anything stupid.

'I've got a clear shot, chief; ready to engage,' one sniper was heard over several radio units, his voice echoing out into the once bustling town which has now diminished into what can only be described as a modern-day ghost town, one of dozens in rural Ireland.

'I just need somewhere to sleep, I've nowhere to go!' the crazed man shouted, striking fear into the hearts of the soldiers now manning the perimeter of a shopping district once called Market Place.

'Step away from the vacant property,' an order was given via megaphone, before correcting, 'no, sorry, not that vacant property, the other … ah, wait, they're all … look, just fuck away from the entire street, will ya? That's some investment fund's asset and we need to protect it even though they're not paying any taxes or rates.'

Standing down as the threat to vacant property prices left the area, some army recruits looked on in envy at the pristine condition of the vacant units compared to the accommodation on their own army barracks.

'I wouldn't blame him for trying,' concluded one soldier.

> **'I've got a clear shot, chief; ready to engage'**

### 2025 Predictions

Confusion will arise after ungrateful renters, in a bid to pressurise Government to change Ireland's planning laws, incorrectly state that small, poorer quality apartments with reduced natural light, no balconies and fewer fire exits aren't the solution to the housing crisis.

# WW news

Waterford Whispers News

**BUSINESS**

Waterford Whispers News

## GAMING

# SONY LAUNCH PLAYSTATION 10 OUT OF FUCKING NOWHERE

SKIPPING four models in a bid to get ahead of any competition, Sony has announced it is to release PlayStation X tomorrow morning 'out of fucking nowhere', *WWN* Tech reports.

The huge leap forward has been met with some controversy as the PlayStation 5 hasn't really been given much air to breathe since its release in November 2020.

'Remember when you were all killing each other trying to get the new PS5 because we drip-fed production causing consoles to be sold for silly money and then you realised it wasn't much of a jump really and felt kind of duped? Well let us introduce the new PlayStation X, which will only be available tomorrow morning between 8.59 a.m. and 9 a.m.,' a spokesperson for PlayStation stated.

It is understood just 1,000 consoles will be sold tomorrow morning at a price of €3,200 each only to people with the name John Smith.

'Obviously skipping four models has its setbacks as this series was originally intended to be released in 2040, so we need to drip feed it,' the statement read, adding, 'also you won't be able to play any games on it for another 15 years as it's so advanced, but we're certain there's a market for it as you idiots will literally buy anything we tell you to.'

Thousands of gamers have already begun camping outside designated stores across the world in the hopes of securing the new console.

'I like game machine,' explained full-time son of two John Smith from Gorey, 'me first to buy … me happy because everyone jealous,' he concluded before clapping his hands together in joy.

### Classifieds

**LUCRATIVE BUILDING CONTRACTS FOR PALESTINE**

US construction firms sought for lucrative building contracts in what will one day be known as 'formerly Gaza'. Contractors must be fairly lax in bookkeeping, morals.
Contact Bibi

Business

## AVIATION

# WATERFORD AIRPORT IN TALKS WITH RYANAIR TO PRETEND IT'S JUST OUTSIDE DUBLIN

NEGOTIATIONS are under way between Ryanair and Waterford Airport to pretend it's just outside Dublin, *WWN* has learned.

The starting point of the first ever Ryanair flight to London in 1985, Waterford Airport is set to receive €12m of funding to extend its runway to allow commercial flights, with officials now engaged in preliminary discussions with the budget airline in the hope of securing flights, but in stereotypical Ryanair fashion.

'Waterford is basically South Dublin when you think about it,' a pitching document leaked to *WWN* read. 'Sure, 'tis only an hour down the road in a twin cam, boi, tourists flying Ryanair won't know any difference and will expect to be dropped off miles from their real destination anyway, so let's get cracking, lads.'

### County Council Notices

Great to see so many phone repair, charity and barber shops popping up all over the city lately; a sure sign we're all on the right path. Crazy how they can keep going without any customers. Fair play.

If classed as a Dublin airport location, house prices in Waterford are expected to triple overnight with the economy soon entering a Dubai level of financial stability.

'This on top of the North Quays; Waterford will look like the bloody video game *Cyberpunk 2077* when we're done with it,' said the document describing the Déise's future, 'albeit without a functioning 24/7 cardiac care unit, but sure look, you can't win everything, boi!'

## SMALL BUSINESSES

# SMALL FAMILY BUSINESS HANDS OVER FIRST BORN TO REVENUE

'BYE Saoirse, Mammy and Daddy love you; just go with the nice bailiffs now, good girl,' restaurant owners Kate and Darren Conaty said, kissing their wailing firstborn goodbye in lieu of an outstanding revenue balance.

Hit with a multitude of hurdles over the past three years, the Black Kettle Café managed to keep itself afloat with many sacrifices, the latest admittedly being the hardest.

'I suppose Revenue has to live too,' Kate reasoned, as bailiffs promised to be back for their second child, Tanya, if the remaining balance isn't paid in 30 days. 'When you think about it, they only get a quarter of everything you make as a business; if you generate 100k a year, they want 23k of that, if you want to pay yourself a salary out of that 100k, they will also want a quarter of that salary too – double whammy – and if you somehow manage to make a profit in between, they'll want 12.5%. It all seems fair to me.'

However, it wasn't all bad news in the world of business, as husband Darren points out.

'Ah, that's great, Shell just posted a $6bn profit last quarter,' the optimistic restaurateur offered, as outstanding energy bills into the tens of thousands of euros lay on the office whiteboard behind him. 'See? there is light at the end of the tunnel.'

151

**Waterford Whispers News**

## NETWORKING

# MAN'S NEW LINKEDIN PROFILE PICTURE CHANGES BUSINESS AS WE KNOW IT FOREVER

STANDING side on to the camera but turning his head to meet its gaze with a relaxed smirk that says, 'and you thought this was going to be a formal business picture devoid of chill vibes', local marketing account manager Ronan Magee has completely changed the way people think about the business world.

'Fuck, Ronan, this could be like an actor's or a comedian's headshot, you'd never know you were managing the account of Ireland's third largest mobile phone network provider, this is off the chain,' remarked stunned coworkers of Magee's at OutsideTheBubble.

'There's a playfulness to the pic that's just like, "what the fuck, are you ALLOWED to do that?",' said coworkers as they gathered around Magee's Macbook, still trying to take in his updated LinkedIn profile.

Magee worked hard to disguise his satisfaction but broke into a wide grin when someone noticed he had not one but two small pins on his round-neck jumper in the photo which supported marginalised communities.

'No one's brought casual Friday/rooftop office pizza party to LinkedIn profile pictures before, it's so countercultural, so non-conformist, wow,' confirmed Ronan of himself, finally feeling ready to admit out loud the staggering levels of formal informality he has ascended to.

UPDATE: Ken in accounts updated his profile picture this lunchtime, sparking Ronan to consider whether it is possible to copyright what is very much his 'personal business brand'.

# URGENT RECALL: MORBEG MEAT FOUND IN BEEF BURGER PRODUCTS ON IRISH SUPERMARKET SHELVES

THE FOOD Safety Authority has urged consumers not to eat any Fahey's Farm branded beef burgers found in a variety of leading supermarkets over fears they may contain morbeg meat.

A Fahey's Farm spokesperson said that an investigation is under way to figure out how this happened but they suspect a herd of morbegs, known as a 'mania of morbegs', may have breached the fences of their farmland and fallen into a tenderiser.

'While morbeg meat is safe to eat, if a little tough and chewy, our customers may on moral grounds feel they can't in good conscience eat a creature capable of teaching basic Irish to young children,' said a Fahey spokesperson.

A rare and endangered species native to Ireland, specifically Morbeg Land, consuming morbeg meat has been illegal since the 1970s due to dwindling numbers but rich Irish clientele have been known to pay restaurants to serve and cook the meat.

The alarm was first raised by a customer who reported finding the sock-like remnants of a morbeg's ear in his stool after eating what he believed was a 100% beef burger.

UPDATE: A Fahey's spokesperson has denied any knowledge of a mass grave found beneath the Growing Tree.

Business

## RECYCLING

# MEET THE BINMEN MAKING MILLIONS FROM RETURNING YOUR RECYCLABLE CONTAINERS

PULLING up to a local housing estate in a Lamborghini refuse truck, binmen Derek Maher and Niall Rogers rubbed their hands with glee, anticipating the cold hard cash they're going to make today from recycle bins packed full of lucrative plastic containers.

'Made my first million last month,' Derek reveals, carefully emptying the contents of number 5 Lime Road into their souped-up bin lorry. 'We could make 10, 20Gs a day – the deposit return scheme changed my life.'

In the first 40 days of the scheme, €1.2m worth of deposits were returned to customers in the form of vouchers issued by reverse vending machines; however, almost €20m in deposits were said to be left unclaimed, sparking a scramble by opportunists.

'It's like the gold rush boy!' said wheelie bin technician Rogers. 'We're fighting for overtime at the moment and working 24 hours a day, searching recycling skips in the refuse centres when we've finished the day job – I bought my first house last week, cash, using deposit return scheme vouchers.'

Refuse companies have been inundated with job applications since the scheme began, with potential employees even offering to work for free just to get a cut of the action.

> 'I bought my first house last week, cash, using deposit return scheme vouchers'

'Hanging on to the back of a truck in the freezing rain used to be a job no one wanted, but now we're having to turn away fellas,' refuse company CEO Jimmy Sacks told *WWN*.

When asked whether spiteful binmen will now be happy enough in their jobs where they don't deliberately leave the bin in the middle of your driveway any more, blocking your entry, the majority said this will never happen as it's too much fun.

**Community Alert**

No.17 haven't cut their grass in forever, it's probably bringing down the houses prices, the state of it.

Waterford Whispers News

## DRIVING TEST
# 70,000 DRIVERS ON WAITING LIST TO TAKE TEST IN ONE LONG CAR

A SOLUTION to the current 70,000-strong waiting list for a driving test in Ireland has been found this morning after the RSA was contacted by the owner of a Waterford garage and limousine service.

'I was on the shitter when it came to me, by welding my fleet of limousines together I'd have one big super car everyone can do their test in at once,' explained Dessie Freel, who admitted all his best ideas, including the driver's seat trapdoor toilet, come to him while he's on the toilet.

The RSA has asked all 70,000 drivers awaiting a test to make themselves available at Blarney Street in Cork city at 9 a.m. this Friday, where all drivers will be tested in one single sitting.

'Blarney Street is the longest residential street in Ireland, and we can't use the M50 obviously, these losers don't have a full licence haha, so the 1.57km Blarney Street it is,' confirmed a spokesperson for the RSA.

'To clear the backlog, we've had to use our ingenuity. But for those nervous test takers, don't worry, everyone will be given their own dedicated curmudgeonly tester who smells of last's week takeaway and has lost their zest for life,' added the RSA.

Impressed by the fresh thinking displayed by the RSA, the HSE is reportedly thinking of solving waiting list issues in the health service by replacing the cold water taps in Irish homes with Calpol.

### Community Alert
Anyone have the number for the lad who did the Reillys' garden? Not looking for work done, just looking to start an affair.

### 2025 Predictions
As part of cost reduction efforts, CEOs will continue to take pay increases while laying off staff.

## ACQUISITIONS

# COFFIN CAM, FINTAN O'TOOLE SIGNING MASS CARDS: HOW RIP.IE WILL CHANGE UNDER *IRISH TIMES* OWNERSHIP

WITH the *Irish Times* purchasing RIP.ie for an undisclosed sum (€3.75bn), many death notice addicts have expressed fear that their beloved pastime could change beyond recognition.

*WWN* has been in touch with *Irish Times* rep Adriana Acosta Cortez, who helped to clear up some misinformation and inform us on what changes are in store for the Taylor Swift of death notice websites:

- Coffin cam – an exclusive camera from inside the deceased's coffin will be available online for a payment of €5 per coffin.
- The Memorial Gifts section of the website will now offer mass cards signed by Fintan O'Toole.
- The property supplement on RIP will showcase the most expensive grave sites in Ireland.
- In an attempt to keep rival death notice websites such as AhJaysusIOnlySawHimLastWeek.ie and IDidntKnowTheyWereIll.ie from gaining further market share, the newspaper said it will keep RIP free to access.
- The 'tea and sandwiches' offer on the site will be replaced with an 'oat latte coffee and deconstructed chicken fillet rolls' premium package.
- An exclusive version of the *Irish Times*' Pricewatch column will appear on RIP, with the words 'how fucking much?' appearing after every quote for funeral director services.
- *Inside Death* will be a daily podcast hosted by the *IT*'s new RIP.ie correspondents, a selection of Ireland's foremost gossiping mams.
- Dublin-based funerals will be given the bulk of the website, with rural notices shoved to the back pages.
- A 'name and shame' page will be set up on the site, ranking the quality of the spreads at funerals.

### Classifieds

**DON'T CARE HOME**

Parents starting to look shook? Are they forgetting simple tasks like not making that substantial will out to you last week? Is their home worth a few bob and you just want to liquidate the asset quickly? Why not try Don't Care Homes today and we can guarantee you a short but profitable solution for all your family needs. Average care to end of life approximately six months.

Don't Care Homes – 'We don't care so you don't have to either'

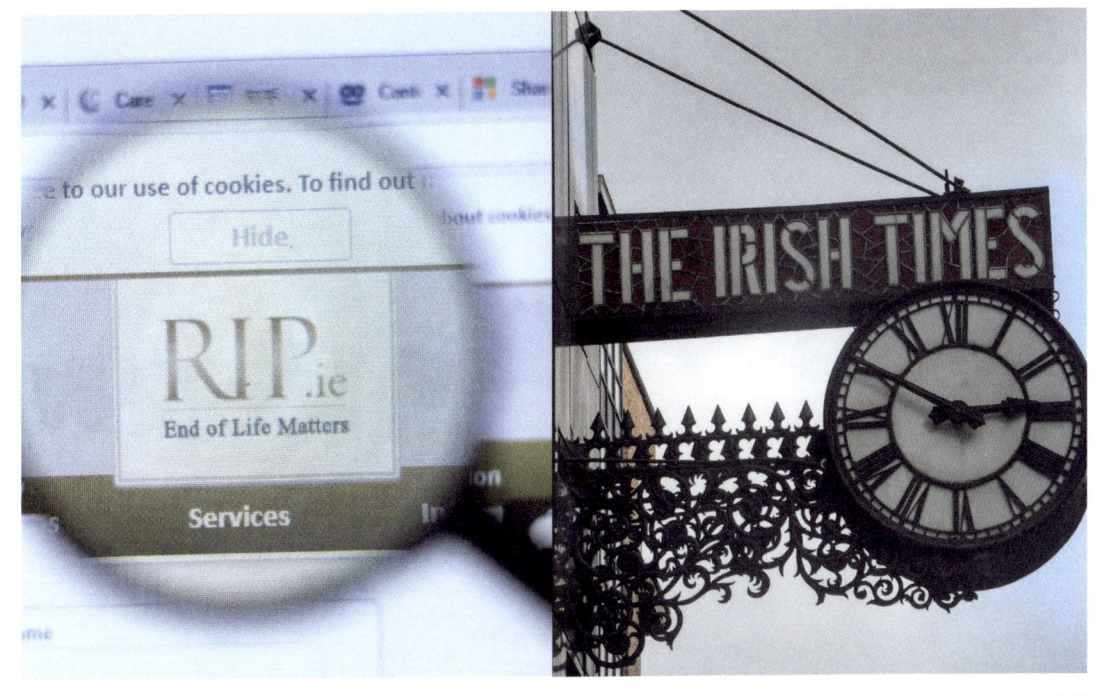

# Waterford Whispers News

## THE TROUBLES

# CONFUSION AS NORDIE CO-WORKER HAS NO TANGIBLE LINK TO THE TROUBLES

AN INTERNAL office investigation, carried out by the co-workers of Tyrone native Henry Childs, has been launched following the revelation that despite being over the age of 50 he has no Troubles-era anecdotes, nor was he interned at Long Kesh or had a relative who was Gerry Adams.

'I'm not buying it, he was MI5 then or something,' remarked lead investigator Tony Roche, whose investigation took the form of whispering with all his co-workers in the cramped office kitchen.

'It's weird, I asked him a question about Semtex and he didn't know the answer, I played some Wolfe Tones on the radio, no strong reaction one way or another,' offered Roche, completely stumped by the walking, talking anomaly that is Childs.

Childs' dearth of salacious tidbits of bomb making or living next door to an IRA safe house has prompted calls for people from Northern Ireland to be more upfront about being boring shites.

'Not even a kneecapped second cousin, it's not on,' receptionist Anna O'Brien stated.

Yet more disappointment had to be endured by Childs' co-workers as he revealed in casual conversation, undertaken by O'Brien with the sole aim of getting 'Troubles dirt' out of the 55-year-old, that he wasn't forced to leave Tyrone on account of an ATM robbery gone wrong and merely moved to Waterford due to work.

> 'I'm not buying it, he was MI5 then or something'

### Did You Know?
CEOs at companies responsible for the majority of the world's pollution are pretty sure this is actually all your fault.

### County Council Notices
Be sure to check out the council's spooky Scareageddon Festival. It's already resulted in three heart attacks, so you know it's good.

'Wait, maybe "work" means IRA stuff,' posited lead investigator Roche, which was a much more plausible explanation for Childs' mind-numbingly boring account of his life.

# BREAKING

## 'PINTS?' BIN REMINDER TEXTS OUT OF NOWHERE

DECIDING to finally take the plunge and bring customer relations to a whole new level, customers of local refuse company Binlads received a single 'Pints?' text last night instead of their usual reminder to put out the black or green bins.

'We understand that our texts are probably the only thing keeping some people going these days so we said fuck it, let's ask if anyone wants to go for scoops,' Binlad's head of communications Cormac Walsh told *WWN*.

Receiving dozens of replies, including 47 Binlads customers who replied yes, a specialised team of pint guzzlers was set up to carry out the proposal. A weekly Tuesday night club was soon forged across the southeast. 'It was a great night out and all and the Binlads are great craic, but I forgot to put out me bloody recycling this morning as I was in such a hoop coming home last night,' local bachelor Larry Ryan (68) told *WWN*.

In a follow-up text the next day, customers who accepted the pints text were greeted with a 'How's the head?' text, followed by, 'I can't remember getting home lol', much to the amusement of everyone.

A similar scheme undertaken by energy suppliers, who texted the same message after issuing a fresh bill, was roundly met with universal 'fuck off' texts from customers.

## TAYTO RELEASE NOISELESS CRISP RANGE FOR WATCHING TV

NOT BEING able to hear the television for the sound of your own munching is probably the most frustrating thing known to mankind, which is why scientists have been developing a noiseless crisp that still feels and tastes the same as the original, but without the annoying crunch.

'This three-billion-euro project is going to revolutionise the way the world watches television and cinema,' lead scientist Professor Paddy Kennedy told *WWN* at Tayto Labs today, demonstrating the new noiseless crisp in a room set up like a typical sitting room with two test subjects watching TV.

'As you can see here, both subject A and subject B are watching TV while eating Tayto's original packets,' he narrated the staged scene as both subjects looked visibly annoyed at their own crunching. 'Now we see the results with the new chip,' he continued, as the emotional pair looked overwhelmed at the lack of munch.

'This changes everything,' subject A told the room, now visibly weeping at the breakthrough. 'To think I was going to leave my wife over this issue and now it has been solved, thank you science, I'll just need to find another excuse now to leave her!'

Tayto confirmed that although the crunching noise will now be obsolete in public areas like cinemas, it will not curtail the number of pricks still talking through movies.

The new noiseless crisp is due to be released in 2024 under the name Tayto Stealth.

---

**Famous Quotes from 2024**

"Are any of you lazy fucks capable of doing any work without my help?"
- ChatGPT

Waterford Whispers News

## WORKFORCE

# GEN Z WORKERS ONLY CAPABLE OF OPERATING IN ONE GEAR, FINDS REPORT

A NEW study into the capability of Gen Z workers has found 99% of them are only able to operate at the one pace, despite whatever demand their role entails.

From deli workers to scientists, people born from the late '90s onwards do not have the concept of working faster during busy times, seemingly trapped in a slow methodical stride without so much as a care in the world.

'All you have to do is go to a busy bar and try ordering a pint,' pointed out lead researcher of the study Professor Kevin Kennedy. 'No matter how quiet or busy the bar is, the Gen Z subject will chug along at the same slow pace without feeling the urge to pick it up a bit in order to, you know,

**2025 Predictions**

Tensions rise between Ireland and China over who invented the spice bag.

serve people quicker and thus deliver a better customer service experience.'

The study found that despite their slow pace and productivity, Gen Z workers still got paid the same as their faster, older colleagues, which was found to have sparked a deep-set resentment towards them across previous generations.

'We'd advise employers to hire two Gen Z workers for any position that requires a faster pace if they want to maintain the efficiency of the olden days of employment,' the report concluded.

A separate study found lazy and workshy people between the ages of 30 and 99 vastly overestimate how efficient and hardworking they are when compared to their Gen Z counterparts.

---

AFTER almost twenty years, Drinkaware.ie is celebrating its fiftieth site hit today in a special ceremony, *WWN* has learned.

Presenting the prize to the fiftieth person to visit the charity's website, County Galway man James Freecastle was presented with a special plaque congratulating him for his visit.

'I was looking for cheap drink ware to buy for the Christmas,' Mr Freecastle told *WWN*, 'to be honest I didn't even remember clicking, what does it do again?'

Drinkaware.ie, a charity funded by the alcohol industry in a bid to do some good while profiting from a drug that is one of the leading causes of death in the known world, thanked the Galway man and his 49 predecessors for their clicks, stating that they are looking forward to the next 50 clicks from concerned Irish drinkers over the next 20 years.

## DRINKAWARE.IE CELEBRATES 50TH WEBSITE VISITOR

'It was at 49 for ages,' a spokesperson for the 'charity' said, recalling the special moment. 'We had to double check the click wasn't just an AI bot trawling the site.' She added, 'that's 50 people in Ireland currently aware about the dangers of alcohol, which makes it all worthwhile.'

Business

## AVIATION

# PROBE DUE AFTER BOEING PLANES FOUND TO BE MADE ENTIRELY OF RECYCLED TOILET PAPER

AIRLINE regulators across the world have launched a probe into plane manufacturer Boeing after it was revealed their aircraft were made entirely from recycled toilet paper.

Boeing confirmed it has been manufacturing commercial aircraft with crusted old toilet paper retrieved from sewerage systems containing the faeces and bodily fluids from millions of people.

'When that stuff dries it's like carbon fibre,' a spokesperson for Boeing said, defending the use of recycled arse wipes. 'I suppose it's a case of what people don't know won't hurt them, but obviously now they know and they're making a storm in a teacup.'

> 'We just want to reassure people flying our planes during these uncertain times that senior executive bonuses remain safe'

'We just want to reassure people flying our planes during these uncertain times that senior executive bonuses remain safe.'

Extracted, dried, and worked into aircraft panels, the 'robust' material is then treated with a special ointment to rid the structure of any odours.

'We also use Weetabix and milk to seal the aircraft,' Boeing expanded on their construction process. 'There's nothing harder than dried-up Weetabix.'

This latest controversy follows a series of Boeing incidents, with the latest being an engine cover falling off a Southwest Airlines flight to Denver.

### County Council Notices

Warning: there's a big important tech conference in town this week. Yanks and everything at it. Don't fuck this up for us. Best behaviour.

### Mindlessness Tip

Throughout your day, it's a good idea to pause for a minute and shut your eyes. This stops the distraction of looking at things around you and makes it easier to draw attention inwards while blocking out the beeps of the other motorists on the M50.

'We will launch a full investigation into this latest incident once we get through the previous several hundred incidents,' the spokesperson stated.

Waterford Whispers News

## RETAIL

# FIRST PENNEYS DRIVE-THRU OPENS IN WATERFORD

FASHION retailer Penneys has launched the company's first ever drive-thru store in Waterford city centre today in a bid to bring even more convenience to customers wishing to make a quick purchase.

Customers will now be able to simply drive up and order low-budget fashion items before moving on to a collection point with the option of trying on the clothes in the comfort of their own cars.

'It's genius really,' Waterford woman Clare Timmons said of the new drive-thru today while purchasing some underwear. 'They even have a returns section so if these don't fit me, I can just hand them back on the way out'.

The new drive-thru will also be open 24 hours, perfect when you need a pair of slippers or a T-shirt that disintegrates after one wash.

The drive-thru also offers a nail bar and eyebrow threading service but customers are warned to keep their handbrake on during the treatment after one customer pushed on the accelerator and lost an eyebrow in the process.

'It's great; I'll literally get all my Xmas shopping done at 2 a.m. on Christmas morning for €15,' one stereotypical man told *WWN*.

> 'It's great; I'll literally get all my Xmas shopping done at 2 a.m. on Christmas morning for €15'

### The Year in Numbers

**100%** Amount of insurance companies raising their premiums despite reduction in payouts.

### Mindlessness Tip

Your heart is precious cargo. And what do we do with precious cargo? Well if you're DPD you drop kick it into the porch with all the delicacy of a bulldozer operating a sewing machine.

# ww news

**Waterford Whispers News**

*WWN* GUIDES

Waterford Whispers News

**CONVERSATION**

# 'YOU'RE ALWAYS OUT, MAURA': A SENIOR WOMAN'S GUIDE TO PASSIVE AGGRESSIVE INSULTS

PUTTING down your fellow senior females is an art form as old as the Earth itself. Passively aggressively throwing digs may seem like an easy thing to do, but it takes decades of bitchiness to perfect.

WWN's self-confessed in-house wagon Peggy Tierney guides you on all the best lines to drop in the hopes of ruining someone's day/night.

### 'You're Always Out, Maura'
Perfect for sending that cow Maura Foley into a hissy fit while she's out enjoying a few drinks and some live music with the husband. Creating the impression that she may have an alcohol dependency is a great way of ruining her evening, the trollop. Watch her scowl as she now purposely takes her time with her Chardonnay in a bid to prove you wrong. Laugh with your friends as you watch Maura then transfer her anger onto her partner before leaving early in a rage, leaving a full glass of fermented grape juice in her wake.

### 'I Didn't Recognise You, Margaret, Were Ya Sick for a While?'
Appearances are everything, so why not play on that by making your target self-conscious. Margaret was once known for her good looks back in the day whilst you were stuck raising a family, so there's no harm in reminding her that she's older now and possibly due an illness of some kind. Make sure to say this line as patronisingly as possible and with a big silly grin on your face.

### 'That Wouldn't be my Cup of Tea now'
Did your neighbour Mary Hennessey get a new car, kitchen or conservatory? Let her know your opinion on it straight away and burst that pretentious bubble of hers. For Christ's sake, Mary, no one has pine presses any more, that's so '90s. Why does your brand-new electric car sound like angels singing, are you preparing to pass over? I suppose you won't see how grotesque the conservatory is from the inside, and it will be worth the eyesore when you're sitting in the heat on those cold winter days.

---

**County Council Notices**

All locals looking to burn down a vacant building must first register their interest with the gardaí.

## FOOD

# ENOUGH WITH THE FUCKING SOURDOUGH, CAFÉS TOLD

**2025 Predictions**
The Children's Hospital will go on a gap year to find itself.

**The Year in Numbers**
0 Number of children named Marty in Ireland this year. An all-time low.

TIRED of being given sourdough as a standard type of bread-based accompaniment with their meals, Ireland's café and restaurant customers have called on owners and chefs to give it a fucking rest already.

'It's like the panini plague of the early noughties when it seemed there was no other type of bread left in Ireland at the time,' one regular café customer recalls. 'If I want stale textured air-bubbled bread I'll ask for sourdough, but otherwise just give me the normal, good old-fashioned sliced pan for now.

'No one wants an Irish breakfast with fecking sourdough – sure the egg yolk falls through the bloody holes, which is absolute madness.'

Noted as a bread for people with notions, sourdough weaselled its way into Irish food menus pre-Covid, before infesting every single café, restaurant and fine dining establishment in the country with its pretentious crust.

'What pisses me off is the bloody muck is neither sour nor doughy,' another normal bread enthusiast pointed out. 'Besides, it's far from sourdough most Irish people were raised – it doesn't even toast nice.'

Meanwhile, bakers have confirmed they're currently deciding on the next big bread fad to flog to the nation.

'We've gone through baguette, pitta, panini, ciabatta, brioche; I think it's time to give rye bread a whirl,' one local baker suggested, before being beaten to death.

Waterford Whispers News

## PETS

# 'MY DOG ATE IT': EXCUSES FOR NOT HAVING YOUR DOG ON A LEAD AFTER IT MAULS ANOTHER DOG

WE'VE ALL been there; you're out walking your pair of unleashed German shepherds when suddenly some old woman with a little shit of a thing on a lead starts yelping for no reason, forcing your boys to defend themselves against its piercing barks. Please find some handy reasons below for not having them on a lead.

**Community Alert**
Renters up the street still haven't cut the lawn. Obviously no regard for actual homeowners. Not married either. Kids are going to Educate Together too. No shame.

**The Year in Numbers**
0 Number of celebrities actually 'cancelled'.

**'My Dogs Ate It.'**
In the same way they ate your dog, they also ate their own leads, hence they're not on one. Duh! Like, what's not to get here? What, am I expected to keep buying them leads just because your dog can't shut up barking? How about control your own dog?

**'It's Cruel to Have a Lead Around a Dog's Neck.'**
I like to treat my dogs with respect, unlike you there, tugging on your tiny mutt's lead almost choking it to death when my two were only running over to tell it to shut up. Once it gets over its PTSD in a couple of years, the dozen or so teeth marks should teach it to stay quiet now when bigger dogs are around. They probably saved its future life. You're welcome.

**'What are you Doing Walking Your Dog at this Time of the Night Anyway?'**
Seriously, I come out at this time of the night so I can leave my dogs off the lead, yet here you are now giving out. I was actually thinking of people like you, so I could avoid you, yet here you are.

**'This is Nature, Dogs Need to Roam Free.'**
I know technically a people's park in the middle of a busy city is not the Burren, but where else am I supposed to let Tyson and Holyfield run around? Last week some soft prick on the beach was giving out because they cornered him, now here you are wailing at me because your dog started a fight, and mine finished it. I can't win.

164

**WWN** Guides

TOILET

# CAUGHT SHORT WITH A TURTLE HEAD? HERE ARE YOUR BEST OPTIONS

THAT old familiar cramp below the navel, the shuddering of your lower extremities and that underlying dread that you are about to soil yourself like a helpless newborn baby; we've all been there, but just what are your options if you're caught short with a huge turtle head of a turd protruding from your anus?

### Pushing It Back In
The second your internal meltdown sirens begin blaring it is essential to first source some kind of implement to plug your exit hole. Everyday objects like old batteries, golf balls or even a Pringles tube can be your friend here, depending on your girth and of course arse contractions. Gently insert said object and casually make your way to your nearest toilet bowl/ditch to unplug.

### Quick Squat and Run
Chancing the old squat-and-run routine can be a tricky one to get away with, especially if caught short in a working scenario like a building site or warehouse where toilets are few and far between. Timing is everything and making sure you practise the jocks pull down and pull up is key to getting away with this.

Find a nice quiet spot like the back of a truck or crate of bananas and pull down, squat, release, pull up and go as quickly as possible to the nearest WC to remove the evidence. Yes, you will have swamp arse for a minute or two, but it beats your last and final resort …

### Just Shitting Yourself
Sometimes you've just got to let nature take its course. Young children do this all the time. Elderly people too. You're allowed to do this at least once in your mid-adult life, so don't be ashamed of it. Proudly just let it swarm your pants. Putting your hands in your pockets and pulling them tight so it doesn't all flow down your legs and onto the floor may get you most of your way to the nearest toilet, but there will be a stage when everyone in the vicinity starts to see the tell-tale markings and get a waft of the putrid odour. The main thing here is to reassure yourself this is fine, there are plenty of other countries in the world you can relocate to.

Waterford Whispers News

## MOVIES

# JOKING DURING A SAD MOVIE SCENE TO STOP YOURSELF FROM CRYING: A GUIDE

SHOWING you're capable of emotion and empathy is probably one of the weakest things you can do as a human being, especially in the comfort of your own sitting room surrounded by friends and family.

In a bid to help avoid such a horrible scenario, WWN has devised this handy guide to inappropriately cracking jokes during the top most tear-jerking scenes in movie history.

### When Mufasa dies in *The Lion King*

People dying in a movie is fine, but by Jesus if you put an animal into the mix, we're all dead from dehydrating eyeballs. *The Lion King* scene when Mufasa gets trampled to death will need some top-tier comedy, so here's a couple of hilarious one-lioners (lolz) to get you through it while everyone else weeps and asks what the fuck is wrong with you.

- 'I hope he had life insurance bahahaha!'
- 'At least Simba doesn't have to fork out for Father's Day now.'
- 'He's just lion there … get it?'

### When John Coffey asks not to have the hood on because he's afraid of the dark when he is about to be executed in *The Green Mile*

Christ, this is a tough scene. Poor bastard gets an awful doing and the scene drags out for a good five minutes so best have a good few zingers for this.

- 'I'd say the electricity bill will be through the roof!'
- 'He won't be awful tired any more hahahahahahaha.'
- 'That's a bit American now, frying an innocent black man to death.'
- 'Tom Hanks will be straight off to Epstein's island after this.'

### When Jack dies at the end of *Titanic*

A classic that still gets you right in the eye sacs, but luckily there's loads of material here when Jack's hanging on at the end that no one has thought about yet.

- 'Sure, there's room for a bus on that thing.'
- 'She obviously just turned 25 so he just let her go.'
- 'You'd want the big coat out in that.'

### When Jojo finds his mother was hanged in *Jojo Rabbit*

Stumped with this one. We'd suggest asking if anyone wants a cup of tea and just leaving the room to bawl to yourself like a newborn child.

WWN Guides

SMALL TALK

# 'BACK TO THE RAIN AGAIN' AND OTHER LINES TO BLURT OUT TO COMPLETE STRANGERS

IN IRELAND it is customary to blurt out nonsensical lines to complete strangers for no apparent reason whatsoever – it's part of our culture. Sometimes it's hard to know what to spontaneously say to someone you've never met in your life, so please find some common one-liners we've compiled below.

**'You Wouldn't Want to Be Dying.'**
This is a perfect quip to relay to anyone waiting in a medical waiting room, queue, or Irish A&E department during winter. Uttered by many people who have actually died waiting, be sure to use this wisely and not in front of someone who is currently dying because of the backlog in HSE waiting lists.

**'Back to the Rain Again.'**
This genius observation is ideal for spouting to a complete stranger when passing each other during a torrential downpour. This will alleviate any confusion as to the current status of the weather. Sometimes people can get confused and not know if it's raining or not. This very line can be used to confirm that yes, it is raining again, in Ireland, a country known for its consistently moist weather patterns.

**'At Least It's Not Raining Anyway.'**
This line is to be used in the exact opposite situation to the previous line. A rarity; treasure this one for the two to three days every year when it's not raining in Ireland.

**'The Fuck You Looking At? Do You Want Your Go?'**
Not every conversation is civil. This line is best kept for when you're sick of people's shite and just want to vent your built-up rage and beat seven shades of excrement out of a stranger, or indeed, get the same number of shades bet out of you, all depending on your fitness level of course, and propensity for extreme violence.

**'Do You Know of Anywhere to Rent?'**
This common phrase is probably the most used of our suggested lines to blurt out to complete strangers. But seriously though, if you do know of anywhere, please DM us.

**'It Won't Be Long Now Till Christmas.'**
Again, another line best used if you want to get the head bet off you in a physical altercation.

**Mindlessness Tip**
Try finally winning the approval of your emotionally stunted father by grunting monosyllabically in his direction as he watches sport on TV.

Waterford Whispers News

## DRINKING

# 4 TIME-CONSUMING DRINKS TO ORDER IN A BUSY BAR AT CLOSING TIME

ORDERING drinks at a busy bar can be a stressful experience for everyone involved, so why not up the ante with these four time-consuming alcoholic beverages that will be sure to send any bar staff member into a fit of anxious rage.

### The Year in Numbers

**7** The number of days remaining in a week, despite a UN resolution to reduce them.

**Irish Coffee**
Best kept as an order ten minutes before the bar closes, why not make your last drink of the night a right bastard of a thing to make, forcing the flow of the entire bar into disarray. Watch as the bar staff frantically look for anything that resembles whipped cream while they curse themselves for turning off the coffee machine too early. Fuck it, order 10 of these like the bar counter isn't 10 deep with baying customers shouting, 'when you're ready' in a passive aggressive manner.

**Bloody Mary**
Choosing a drink dependent on a tiny bottle of Tabasco that has been floating around the bar since Italia '90 is a sure-fire way to keep those barmen and -women on their toes. Insist on a leek, making it clear that a poorly chopped spring onion won't do. Cracked pepper only and can I have freshly pulped tomato juice please, none of that stuff in the bottle from the bottom shelf there that has sedimented into layers from standing too long, thanks.

**Irish Whiskey**
Laugh as the barman has to wash the only three handled glasses the bar has in stock while he sends some poor member of floor staff out to the 24-hour for fucking cloves. Are those lemons washed? I didn't think so, you pubs never wash lemons. Can I have five cloves neatly placed in every segment. Where's the perfectly folded napkin around the handle, you heathen? Come on, chop chop, Pavel, this is Ireland, pal, we love Irish whiskeys.

**23 Baby Guinnesses**
Hey, I know a brilliant shot that's as weak as a packet of wine gums and as annoying as a wino with no gums eating a stale baguette – baby Guinness! It's so fun because it's like a mini pint of Guinness and just as painful to make. Is that teaspoon clean? Jesus, you made a right sticky mess of the bar counter there, chief. Can you bring them over to the table please? Man, we're going to be so twisted after drinking one of these 30cl low percentage shots for €6 a pop. Let's drink them in sync like they don't taste like those dark chocolate liquor sweets your weird English aunty sends you for Christmas. Make a disgusted grimace like a hard man would do drinking moonshine. Classic, lads!

### 2025 Predictions
The Wild Atlantic Way is renamed Mild Atlantic Way due to climate change.

## HOUSESHARING

# SIGNS YOU'RE THE LEAST FAVOURITE HOUSEMATE

HOUSESHARING has its pros and cons, but one thing is for sure; it can suck harder than a Henry the Hoover bitten by Dracula if you get the feeling that you are loathed by your housemates.

But just how can you be sure you're the least favourite housemate? Read on to find out.

- The secret WhatsApp group you're not in sees your housemates' phones regularly ping in unison followed by muffled laughter.

**Famous Quotes from 2024**

"Oh God sorry, my phone was on silent and only seeing these now" – **Dee Forbes on all the missed calls and texts from the Oireachtas Committee**

- Your mere entrance into a communal space is more effective at clearing a room than a farting corpse.
- There is little accommodation given to your recent foray into the entrepreneurial field of dealing drugs from the house.
- You begin to suspect your nickname 'The Burden' is less complimentary than it first appeared.
- Housemate drinks always seem to line up with when you've gone back home for the weekend.
- You've been living under the stairs like Harry Potter for several years despite a high turnover of housemates and the largest bedroom being up for grabs.
- You bring back 18 people at 4 a.m. on a Monday night and it's like you strangled a puppy.
- The cleaning rota always seems to end up with you cleaning the bathroom when the toilet is clogged. You're even forced to clear out the sink that still has that shit you did in it.
- Your unrefined loutish housemates have no appreciation for your monthly toe-clipping sessions in the kitchen.
- Perhaps the handwritten 'Eviction Notice but just for The Burden' slipped under your door may not have come directly from the landlord.
- Deirdre can run two washes in the one day but you never hear the end of it about electricity bills when you install a grow house in the attic.

**County Council Notices**

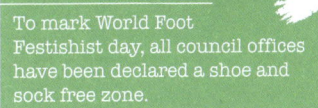

To mark World Foot Festishist day, all council offices have been declared a shoe and sock free zone.

Waterford Whispers News

**PETS**

# CHOOSING THE PERFECT DOG TO MASK THE SMELL OF DOG FROM YOUR BACHELOR PAD

DOES your bachelor pad reek of wet dog, but you don't own a dog and it basically just smells of you? Purchasing an actual dog to disguise the fact you smell like one is your only man.

**Choose a Long-Haired Dog**
You'll need a dog with long, matty hair that when left unwashed smells like a coming-down-off-base-speed Galway crusty after a three-day free party in the woods, which is the perfect dog if you're a coming-down-off-base-speed Galway crusty who tends to regularly go to three-day free parties in the woods.

**Mindlessness Tip**
Maybe stop drinking alcohol every night of the week, you complete fucking mess.

**Incontinent Rescue Dog**
Does your pad smell like old pee and shite? Purchasing an ageing rescue dog who is unable to retain urine or faeces in the body is the perfect choice for you. Friends complaining about the smell of stale piss coming from the wardrobe you drunkenly slashed on while sleepwalking one night? That's the fucking dog mate. Rescue, innit!

**Dead Dog**
Masking your victims' rotting body parts that you carelessly left scattered around the house will never be an easy one to excuse, but it's no problem with a dead dog. Dead dogs can be found anywhere and are relatively cheap too. Dead dogs are low maintenance, don't need walking and make the perfect excuse for dead people smells. Why do you have a dead dog in your flat, they may ask. Just tell them you're finding it hard to let go.

**County Council Notices**
We're hiring! Do you have experience in taking months to get back to an email with a fairly straightforward query? Consider working for the council!

## MOTORING

# CHOOSING THE PERFECT PICKUP TRUCK YOU'LL NEVER PROPERLY UTILISE

ARE you looking for the perfect 3.0-litre pickup truck to help you ferry the odd middle-aisle power tool from Lidl or potted plant like some kind of rugged off-grid bourbon-drinking lumberjack from Alaska? *WWN* Motoring has you covered.

### Size
Could a small hatchback car provide all your future transport needs? Sure, but owning a huge American-style pickup truck looks class and everyone will be like, 'Jaysis, the size of that yoke, he must be like building difficult stuff with his bare hands and probably has big man calluses and everything and probably eats raw meat too.' We suggest opting for the largest sized engine to carry your 20kg bag of coal because you're not going to risk struggling with the bigger bag in case you look weak and puny.

### Colour
Choosing a dark colour pickup is a great way of showing your masculine side; however, we believe purchasing a white pickup can also have some great benefits. Driving a white pickup really gives the impression that you're comfortable with your sexuality, leaving people to speculate that you bought this monstrosity for practical reasons and not just for show. Adding a huge fuck-off bull bar and set of spotlights can up the masculinity a bit if you are slightly worried that driving a spotless white pickup truck that has never ventured on a road with a middle grass divide may get you a slagging from the lads.

### Electric or Diesel?
Really? Are you actually contemplating some kind of fully electric or hybrid version of a pickup truck? Get off our page, you Silk Cut 100-smoking, green-tea-drinking, Sunday-cycling, falafel-eating, *Guardian*-reading snowflake.

---

**Did You Know?**

Ireland is currently experiencing a mass delusion event in which people think the MetroLink will be built on time and within budget.

---

**Classifieds**

**HELP WANTED –
REPORT MY MOTHER'S FACEBOOK ACCOUNT**

I'm looking for dozens of people to report my mother's Facebook account so she gets banned indefinitely. She keeps commenting on every single post she sees and ends up arguing for hours on end with people she has never met. She is becoming a real embarrassment.

Email Dave@hotmail.co.uk

Waterford Whispers News